NO ORDINARY LIFE

LYNCH

History, myth and legend

RONAN LYNCH

First published in Ireland in 2014 by
NO ORDINARY LIFE
57 Clontarf Road
Dublin 3
Ireland
MAIL: editor@noordinarylife.ie
WEB: noordinarylife.ie

A CIP record for this title is available from the British Library.

ISBN
9780993061226

THE LYNCH STORIES

As a child, I had a friend called Murphy, and I admired his luck at having such a fine name. The Murphy clan had given the world 'Murphy's Law' and timeless, verifiable insights into human nature such as 'the other line always moves faster'. Even my own American relatives left Ireland clutching tea towels inscribed with Murphy's Law. I had inherited the surname Lynch and its Gaelic equivalent Loingseach (or sometimes Loinseach). In the first year of school, we learned the story of Labraid Loinseach, the king with horses' ears. This story inspired a chant very much enjoyed by my five-year-old classmates: "Labraid Loinseach has horses' ears, Labraid Loinseach has horses' ears." It all seemed unfair. Why did my family have such a stupid legend? Why couldn't we have a witty, amusing law, like Murphy?

We did in fact have a law, but I didn't hear about it until I was well out of primary school, and it wasn't the type of thing one printed on tea towels and sold to tourists, or at least not in Ireland. 'Lynch's law' was named for the vigilante-style punishment beating or killing that evolved into the widespread illegal killing of poor black Americans during the nineteenth and twentieth centuries. As a student I had an interest in basketball and American football and noticed that there were a number of black athletes with the Lynch surname. How, I wondered, were there were so many black Lynches in America? Many black Americans had inherited their family names from plantation owners and slaveholders, but according to the history

4

that we learned in Irish schools, we Irish were victims of colonisation, not its perpetrators. We weren't the type of people who owned slaves or plantations. As it turned out, we had learned one particular version of history, where mythology competed with historical reality. I would come to discover that the descendants of the wealthy Lynch family of Galway did indeed own plantations, and slaves. The privilege of European emigrants extended to the Gaelic Lynches who had made their way to the Caribbean or the southern states, and had also owned slaves.

The name Lynch, unusually, has unrelated Irish, English and Anglo-Norman origins and down through the centuries, there have been three distinct branches of the family sharing the same name. The English Lynch family is by far the smallest branch. In Ireland, the family is split into those with Gaelic Irish origins, and a branch of Anglo-Norman origin which has long been associated with the Lynch family of Galway.

It's likely that the family name of these Anglo-Normans started with one man who arrived to Ireland as a mercenary in the service of the Anglo-Norman invaders of the 12th century, and it's this branch of the family that has written itself most effectively into history. This family first settled on Ireland's east coast as mercenaries travelling with Strongbow and the other Anglo-Norman invaders, and soon became merchants on the west coast, taking their place as one of the 'tribes' that ruled Galway for several centuries, taking their trade up and down the European coast and eventually west to the Caribbean.

When the Lynch family began their move across the Atlantic, they did so in two waves, reflecting the two origins of the Irish branch of the family. The merchant Lynches of Galway were in the first wave, which was well underway by the 17th century; the second wave was the Gaelic Lynches, who were mostly forced into emigration by famine and lack of opportunity. The Lynches are one of the biggest Irish tribes in the US, surpassed in number only by the tribes of Burke, Morris, Murphy, Kelly, Sullivan, Coleman, Ward, Reynolds, Ryan, Dunn, Cunningham, Carroll, and O'Brien. The US census of 2000 showed more than 100,000 Lynches living in America. Of these, 84% declared themselves to be White, 11% were Black, 1.7% were of Hispanic origin, 1.6% were of 'Non-Hispanic of Two or More Races', almost 1% were American Indian or Alaskan Natives, and .43% identified themselves as Asian and Pacific Islanders. Lynch is the 237th most popular name in America, so from every 100,000 Americans, one can expect to find 42 or 43 Lynches. Lynches have settled all around the world, with many more living outside Ireland than in Ireland.

So, as a family with a thousand years of history behind them and descendants around the world, the Lynches are the subject of many stories, myths and legends. This book investigates the extent to which stories are based in fact or fiction. One way of looking at history is to consider that facts deal with truths that can be verified. Legends, meanwhile, are stories handed down over the ages that often have their roots in some true story, with layers of detail that have been added over time. Myths are stories, often without any roots in truth, that can hint at deeper truths. Put it this way: a myth will almost always have deeper meaning that a fact.

Take for instance the story of the Mayor of Galway who hanged his own son. The legend of the Mayor of Galway has some basis in fact. There are real characters and real events in the story of the Mayor, but the story itself was most likely created to fulfil the need to cast the Lynch family as faultlessly law-abiding, and the story resonates with similar stories going back to the days of Abraham and his efforts to appease God by sacrificing his son Isaac.

How about the story of lynching? One story traces the phrase to a cruel and conniving slave master called Willie Lynch, and this story of Willie Lynch resonated strongly with black Americans in the 1990s. As we'll see, Willie Lynch was an invented character, but the word 'lynching' does indeed come from another Lynch of the southern US. How many people know the story of Grayston Lynch, the CIA man who inspired the Colonel Lynch of popular TV series *The A–Team*, who spent his days fighting another famous Lynch, better known as Che Guevara?

How about the story of the US soldier Jessica Lynch, who was captured by enemy forces during the invasion of Iraq in 2003, and was dramatically rescued by US troops? She briefly became an icon of US military bravery, and the story of her brave family became equally famous, even though it later turned out to have been largely imagined by a *New York Times* reporter called Jason Blair. As the months went by following Jessica Lynch's return to the United States, she began to tell reporters that her story was more about show business and public relations than about any bravery on her part.

Indeed, with the spread of media into every nook and cranny of our lives in the always-on modern world, it's not surprising that the most well-known Lynches are no longer adventurers, mercenaries or merchants but entertainers, filmmakers, actors, singers and sports stars. Still, even in this arena, we have modern masters who navigate not seas but worlds of perception.

Finally, there are many places, concepts and objects associated with the name Lynch: we have Lynchian as an adjective and Lynch Syndrome as a condition; there are the Lynch wines and there is whisky from Lynchburg; there are Lynchburgers (actual hamburgers) from Seattle and Lynchburgers from Lynchburg, Virginia and Lynchburg, Tennessee. Then there's the city of Linz in Austria, which in one legend is the origin of the Lynch family name, and a place that Adolf Hitler once planned to turn into a world capital under the most bizarre of circumstances.

In historical terms, original records fall to pieces or are lost or simply recede into the mists of time. Yet the internet has allowed persons of common ancestry to share their personal family histories.

Using modern technology, people can build up a picture of a family from diverse circumstances and places and join together to share what they may have previously thought of as information only of interest to themselves. Additionally, the digitisation of old records is an extraordinary tool for researchers, and allowed me to trace the early origins of the Anglo-Norman Lynches by searching digitally through great volumes of records.

This book aims to draw no broad conclusions about the greater Lynch family, even though we can amuse ourselves by looking for patterns. That's part of our psychological make up, but any historian soon realises the futility, not to say comedy, of trying to fit human life into a convenient narrative. This book is the story of one family's stories about itself. If anything, it shows how the powerful get to write their own narratives, and the irresistible urge to leaven the unsalted facts of everyday life with the spice of legend, myth and mystery.

THE LEGEND OF LABRAID LOINGSEACH

Lebor Gabála Érenn, or the Book of Invasions, was first compiled in the 11th century, collecting tales and poems that told of the mythological origins of Ireland. The book tells how all Irish people are descended from Noah, and begins with an account of the arrival of Noah's daughter Cessair to Ireland. Until the twentieth century, the *Lebor Gabála Érenn* was widely accepted as the definitive account of the origins of the Irish peoples, and it served as the source for histories of Ireland into the 19th century. By the twentieth century, mainstream scholars had come to accept the *Lebor Gabála Érenn* as pseudohistory, or history that accepts myths and legends as literal truth.

Although discredited as the basis of history, the myths and legends stay with us, for they have much to say about humanity. The story of Labraid Loingseach from the *Lebor Gabála Érenn* relates that the origin of the name Loingseach comes from the word mariner or exile, which in turn comes from the Irish word for ship, 'long'. According to the *Lebor Gabála Érenn,* the story is set in the third century BC.

Labraid was the grandson of High King of Ireland Léogaire Lorc. Legend tells that Léogaire's brother Cobthach the Meagre was consumed with jealousy of the king. Pretending to be mortally ill, Cobthach lured King Léogaire to his deathbed and stabbed him. Cobthach then arranged to poison the king's son Ailill Áine. According to this tale, Cobthach wasn't satisfied with merely poisoning the son, but insisted on torturing his king's grandson, forcing him to eat a portion of the heart of his murdered father and grandfather, and swallow a mouse. The traumatised son was struck dumb by this cruelty, becoming as quiet as a mouse. He was unable to speaking for several years, until he was struck on the leg during a hurling game and cried out "I am hurt", earning him the name 'Labraid', or 'he speaks'.

Soon after the young man's voice returned, he was exiled from Ireland, earning the name 'Loingseach', for exile or mariner. In one version of his exile, from *The Book of Leinster*, tells that King Cobthach asked the court at Tara to name the most generous man in Ireland. The king's poet and the royal harper Craiftine answer 'Labraid' and the king angrily sent all three men into exile.

Initially, Labraid is merely exiled as far as Munster in the south of Ireland where he is taken under the protection of King Scoriath, only for the King's daughter Moriath to fall in love with Labraid. The Queen sleeps with one eye open to keep watch over her daughter, but the harper Craiftine plays a lullaby on his harp that sends the woman to sleep, allowing Moriath and Labraid to consummate their love. The Queen soon realizes she has been deceived, but Labraid confesses and marries Moriath to preserve the family honour. Labraid then travels to France where he spends a further 30 years in exile before returning to Leinster, where he makes peace with his former tormentor Cobthach.

Yet the peace between Labraid and Cobthach breaks down, and they go to war. Labraid spends an entire year building a fortress of iron, and then invites Cobthach and 30 other kings to the fortress to feast. Cobthach arrives with the 30 kings and 700 followers, but refuses to enter the fortress until Labraid's mother and court jester go in before him. Once everyone has entered, they feast and drink ale, but Labraid gets out unnoticed and chains the doors shut, before burning down the fortress, killing everyone inside including his own mother, who has agreed to die to avenge her son's honour.

Despite or perhaps because of the fantastically violent nature of this story, it's a more mundane tale about Labraid Loingseach that is better known, and in this story Labraid is firmly established as a king. This is the story of the King with Horse's Ears, for Labraid had a secret: he had horse's ears and wore his hair long to hide them. Once every year, a barber was chosen at random to cut the king's hair, and was put to death immediately afterwards to preserve the secret. One year, the only son of a widow was chosen, and knowing her son's fate, the woman beseeched the King to spare his life. The king agreed, as long as the son kept the secret for the rest of his life. The barber duly cut the king's hair, and noticed the horse's ears, but the burden of keeping the king's secret started to affect him. Gradually he grew so ill that a local druid advised him to share the secret with another living being, and sent the barber into the forest to seek out a recipient for the secret. The barber told the story to a willow tree deep in the forest, and felt the burden lifted from him.

Not long after, the king's harper Craiftine broke his harp, and set out into the forest to select wood for a new harp. He cut down the willow tree that held the barber's secret and fashioned it into a harp. When he first played it at the royal court, the harp sang out 'Labraid Loingseach has horse's ears!' The court fell silent and everyone looked at Labraid, who realized that his secret was lost. The king started to laugh, followed by his courtiers, and Labraid repented for the death of all of the barbers he had killed.

In the story of the King with Horse's Ears, Labraid murders several innocents but the violence in this tale pales in comparison with the early story where he burns hundreds of people alive. While the story of torture, exile and murder is set in Ireland, the story of the King with Horse's Ears seems to be an Irish variation on a myth that was known in several parts of the world. Although King Midas is known as the man who turns everything he touches to gold, he also had another distinguishing features: ass's ears. After praying for the

11

ability to turn everything to gold, Midas found himself starving because his food turned to gold when he went to bring it to his mouth. Once he had reversed the spell, Midas threw off his love of riches and took to the countryside, where he found himself called upon to judge a musical battle between Pan and Apollo. Alone among the judges, Midas found Pan to be a better musician than Apollo, and his atrocious taste was rewarded by having his ears turned into ass's ears. At this point the story follows a familiar narrative, with Midas's barber confessing the secret at the river, and the river reeds then singing the song to the people.

Sadly we don't know if Labraid Loingseach earned his horse's ears with a similar tone deafness.

FROM LINZ TO LYNCH?

How does a family get its name? You may have heard that old expression that there are only two certain things in life: death and taxes. The introduction of taxation presented administrators with a problem. In a town with a handful of men all named John, Paul or George, it was impossible to tell who had been accounted for and who had escaped the tax net. The answer: make people take a second name. In England, the first poll taxes were introduced in the 14th century, and people were instructed to take names based on their complexion or hair colour (Brown, Black, White), size (Short, Long), trade (Butler, Cook, Cooper, Miller, Smith, Tailor, etc.) or town (Chester). It was 1468 before Edward IV compelled the citizens of Galway to take a second name.

Ireland was one of the first countries to introduce family names, though it was for purposes of prestige rather than taxation. The name O'Cleirigh is recorded in 916 in the *Annals*, derived from clerk. Irish family names used the custom of 'son of' or 'daughter of'. Mac as in MacNiall indicated 'son of' while Ua or O, as in O'Brian, often indicated the grandson or descendant. The Lynch family of Ireland, unusually, has two distinct origins that are differentiated by class and nationality. One branch of the family named O'Loingsigh or O'Loinsigh was in Ireland from pre-Norman times and variations on the name Ó'Loingsigh appear 22 times between 965 and 1165 in the *Great Book of Irish Genealogies*. The *Great Book* was compiled in 1649-50 in Galway by the scholar Dubhaltach Mac Fhirbhisigh, and

13

contained genealogies from both Gaelic and Anglo-Norman families, though the Anglo-Normans disappeared from the record in later genealogies that stressed Gaelic Irish pedigrees.

In her 1925 book, *Lynch Record: Containing biographical sketches of men of the name, Lynch, 16th to 20th century*, Elizabeth Lynch traces several branches of the Lynch family descended from various kings of Ireland. For instance, she names one of the Lynch forebears as Longseach who died in 923, and lays out his genealogy as the twentieth descendant of Fiacha Araidhe, the 37th king of Ulster. Despite the preponderance of Longseachs and Loingseachs in Ireland of the first millennium, a new Lynch family arrived to Ireland early in the second millennium and proceeded to write themselves into the historical record as early as the 12th century, in the records of the Abbey of St. Thomas.

This other branch of the Lynch family came to Ireland in the 12th century though the family claims that England was merely a stopover and that they had arrived in England with William the Conqueror in the 11th century. While I'll often refer to these Lynches of Galway as the aristocratic Lynches, this is in reference to the fact that these soldiers of fortune turned merchants raised themselves to become de facto aristocrats, owning vast tracts of land in the west of Ireland and elsewhere and controlling local administration over the course of several centuries.

It's no accident that the history of Galway's ruling families, including the Lynches, is so well recorded. Since ancient times, rulers have sponsored artists, writers and poets to record their histories and to sing their praises and ensure that their names are remembered for posterity. Several years ago, I wrote a book about the Kirwan family of Castlehacket. The Kirwans were one of the merchant tribes of Galway, but they were the only tribe family to lay claim to Irish origins. The Castlehacket Kirwans had a chequered history. The great 17th century merchant Sir John Kirwan had been known in the countryside as 'the ruin of poor people'. Although the family became close to Protestant Evangelists in the 19th century, they were celebrated in song and folklore as 'good landlords'. On close investigation, it became clear to me that the Kirwans had a keen understanding of local folklore and mythology, and had written themselves into those stories as being favoured by the local 'fairy king' for their generosity towards local people. By the late 20th century, historians had elevated the value of 'folk history' to a place alongside the previously more prestigious records of church and state, and the Kirwans' investment in folk history paid off.

While the Lynches of Galway did not lay claim to the adoration of ordinary people, they've been no less adept at staking their own claim to historical significance. Certainly, they have left their mark on Galway with the 15th or 16th century Lynch townhouse still occupying a prominent position in the city centre, and the family made a wealth of material available to the author of the popular 19th century *History of the Town and County of Galway*. James Hardiman's book remains a major source of information on the tribe families of Galway and has had a great influence on later historians. It is widely quoted in most histories of Galway.

James Hardiman was born around 1790 in Westport, Co. Mayo, where his father owned a small estate. He studied law in Dublin and became an administrator of public records at Dublin Castle, but retained a deep interest in the history and folklore of the west of Ireland. Hardiman was personally acquainted with some of the Lynch families, and when word went around that Hardiman was researching and writing a history of Galway, unnamed persons from the Lynch clan furnished Hardiman with family histories and pedigrees. Hardiman devoted a chapter of his work to the 'tribes of Galway', based on the families who ruled the town for several centuries, and the Lynch family pedigrees became a major source of his work on the family. By the 19th century, the Lynch family of

Galway had split into myriad clans: Their ancestors had served as mayors, provosts and bishops of Galway and family members such as the 18th century soldier Isidore Lynch had commissioned their own pedigrees, as was common among wealthy merchant or aristocratic families. It was the extensive wealth of the Lynch family that allowed them to effectively write themselves into history through Hardiman's book. The variety of information slightly overwhelmed Hardiman, who elected to include all accounts of the Lynch family origins that he thought reasonable. He also included several accounts that he clearly thought to be mythical, but were interesting enough to warrant inclusion in footnotes. At the risk of contradicting himself, Hardiman often threw several versions of a story into the mix.

According to Hardiman, the Lynch family records stated that they were originally from "Lintz, the capital of upper Austria, from which they suppose the name to have been derived; and that they claim descent from Charlemagne, the youngest son of the Emperor of that name". Linz was a Roman settlement on the river Danube, the longest river is Western Europe and was known until the early 9th century as Lentia, named for its position on a bend in the river. It's likely that the Roman settlement had earlier origins, for the local region had been settled since the Neolithic period. The discovery of Bronze Age urns in the nearby area of Hallstatt in the 19th century gave rise to the idea that this region was the origin of Celtic culture. (So, ironically, the Lynches of Lintz may not have been the first locals to make their way to Ireland. It's at the outer realms of possibility but the O'Loinsigh family may also have originated in this region, a millennium or two earlier.)

Whatever about the claim of Austrian origins, the claim of descent from Charlemagne was doubtful. The D'Arcy family and the Burke family also claimed this lineage but the claim of the Burke family seems real; the D'Arcy connection is less certain, as is that of the Lynch family. Charlemagne, Charles the Great, King of the

Franks, was crowned Holy Roman Emperor by Pope Leo III in 800, and ruled over an entity roughly covering the modern states of France and Germany. (There is a real if flimsy connection between Charlemagne and Linz, for in 771 King Charles married Hildegard, daughter of Count Gerold of Vinzgau, and Gerold was given tenure of St. Martin's Church in Linz.)

Regardless of the claim of descent from Charlemagne, which seems unlikely given the relatively well documented fate of his offspring, the Lynch claim of origin from Linz rests also on the family crest; the story of the origins of the crest are linked to the family's claims to have governed the town. According to Hardiman once more: "They also state that the Lynches obtained their armorial bearings from the following circumstances, one of their name and family, being governor of Lintz, (long before the invasion of England by the Conqueror), defended that city with unexampled fortitude, against a powerful enemy; and though from the uncommon length of the siege, all their provisions were consumed, and the garrison reduced to the miserable extremity of subsisting on the common herbage of the fields, he was finally victorious. His prince, amongst other rewards of his valour, presented him with the trefoil on a field azure, for his arms, and the Lynx, the sharpest sighted of all animals, for his crest, the former, in allusion to the extremity to which he was driven for subsistence during the siege, and the latter, to his foresight and vigilance, and, as a testimonial of his fidelity, he also received the motto, semper fidelis, which arms, crest, and motto, are borne by the Lynch family to this day."

These claims of Linz–ian origin and Charlemangian descent seem far fetched but there are reasons for the claims. The continental branch of the family first arrived to Ireland with the name De Lench or De Linch, suggesting that the family did arrive from some place that sounds like Lench or Linch; such places are not readily identifiable in France, apart from Lyon. In the 11th and 12th century, family names were rare and pointed to places of origin so it is indeed possible that the family originated in Linz, Austria, and migrated northwards through France during the 9th and 10th centuries, eventually joining up with William the Conqueror in the 11th century in the invasion of England.

The claim of descent from Charlemange is doubtless false but throws light on the awkward fact that the 19th century Lynches did not feel truly Irish. Some of this was of their own making, for they considered themselves English up until at least the 17th century. As a result, they were not included in the myriad Gaelic pedigrees that became popular in the late 19th century. One source of these Irish pedigrees is the scholar John O'Hart who produced *Irish Pedigrees: The Origin and Stem of the Irish Nation*, followed in 1884 by *The Irish and Anglo–Irish Landed Gentry*, and these books drew heavily on earlier sources such as aforementioned *Great Book of Irish Genealogies*. O'Hart's pedigrees of the Irish people accept the claim that the Irish people descend from Milesius, King of Spain and 36th lineal descendant of Adam. In O'Hart's pedigrees, Milesius came to Ireland in 500BC though we know now from archaeological studies that Ireland was populated several millennia earlier than O'Hart suggests and we also know that O'Hart's lineages prior to 1600AD are suspect. O'Hart's lineages were political and he declined to offer lineages to the Anglo–Normans settlers, although the Anglo–Normans proved to be capable of their own inventions. Where the heralds previously inserted Irish kings, queens and princes into Irish lineages, the Anglo-Normans inserted Irish, English and European kings and princes into their lineages, hence the Lynch claim of descent from Charlemagne.

Admitting all of these various claims of the Lynch family, though relegating most to the footnotes, Hardiman attempted to establish his own version of the Lynch story. Citing the pedigrees in the herald's office, Hardiman traces the family origins to William le Petit, a knight of Hugh de Lacy, and alternatively to a John de Lynch. According to

Hardiman, William Le Petit came to Ireland with Hugh de Lacy in 1185, and had a son Nicholas who was the ancestor of Thomas de Linche, the first of the Lynches of Galway. This assertion comes from William Playfair's *British Family Antiquity* of 1586, with Playfair listing 10 generations from William le Petit to Thomas Lynch, and can be dismissed as there is only a 100 year period from the Anglo-Norman invasion to the days of Thomas de Linche. However, we are arriving at something close to the truth, and it's not unusual that the accounts have become muddled over a period of seven or eight centuries. It's quite certain that the Lynches descended not from de Lacy but from one of his knights whose Latin name was Leonisius de Bromiard. To understand how the Lynch family came to arrive in Ireland with the conquering Anglo-Normans, it's necessary to go back to the turn of the first millennium. From the late 8th century, Normandy in the northwest of France was subjected to waves of raids from the Norsemen, the Vikings of modern-day Denmark and Norway, who began to settle in Normandy in the 9th century, establishing a powerful domain under the Viking Rollo, whose descendants were the first Dukes of Normandy. In the early to mid-11th century, Rollo's great-great-great-grandson William, known as William the Conqueror, had consolidated his power in the area and was a contender for the throne of England. When Harold, Earl of Wessex took the throne in 1066, William invaded England and defeated King Harold's army at the Battle of Hastings. William ushered in the Norman age in England, parcelling out land to his knights, including Walter de Lacy.

De Lacy was granted lands on the England-Wales border in the regions of Herefordshire and Shropshire, which were lost by his son Gilbert but regained by his grandson Hugh de Lacy. One of the towns in Herefordshire is named Bromyard, and it's in connection with the town of Bromyard that we first encounter the name Leonisius, who probably was the forebear of the Anglo-Norman

Lynch family of Ireland. The name "Leonisius de Bromiard" appears in 12th century Irish documents relating to lands in the region of Trim, which was de Lacy's stronghold. It is quite likely therefore that Leonisius was a follower of the Norman de Lacy family, either as a knight or soldier of fortune. Whether Leonisius and his family originated in Normandy or beyond remains unresolved, although as already mentioned, the family did claim origins in Linz of Austria. This we cannot confirm, but the origins of Leon of Bromyard are written into the early church records in Ireland.

In 1169, almost 100 years after the Norman takeover of England, a dispute arose between the King of Leinster Diarmuid MacMorrough and Rory O'Connor, the High King of Ireland. Dispossessed of his kingdom, MacMorrough sought help from King Henry II, who granted MacMorrough permission to request help from the Anglo-Norman lords. The first of the Anglo-Norman lords arrived in 1169, with Richard de Clare, the Earl of Pembroke (also known as Strongbow), leading another force in 1170. Strongbow succeeded in installing himself as King of Leinster. In 1171, Hugh de Lacy sailed for Ireland with King Henry, and was granted the lordship of the rich land of Meath, with the service of fifty Knights. De Lacy and his son William set about building Trim Castle, the greatest of the Irish castles, which still dominates the town.

In exchange for the military service of their knights, the overlords granted land known as 'knight's fees'. Ten kilometres south of Trim, Leonisius de Bromiard was awarded his own domain, which centred around the low hill known as Cnoc an Línsigh or Hill of the Lynches. The town is now better known by its English name of Summerhill. Almost all of what we know about the Lynches of this time comes from the 12th century manuscripts known as the Register of the Abbey of St. Thomas in Dublin, which records grants made to local churches. Leonisius de Bromiard granted several parishes including

Kiltale, Derrypatrick, Culmullin and Kilmore to the monks of the Abbey of St. Thomas in Dublin. We can place these grants taking place shortly before the end of the 12th century, as the grant was confirmed by Eugenius, Bishop of Meath, who died in 1191.

The Register of the Abbey of St. Thomas in Dublin is written in Latin, and the earliest mentions we have of the Lynch forebears is Leonisius of Bromiard, followed by Johannis Filii Leonisis or John son of Leon. Johannis Filii Leonisis becomes known as John Fitz Leon, or John Fitz Leones. Local lore in Summerhill regards the Lynch family name as having descended from the FitzLeons or FitzLeones, the descendants of Leonisius of Bromiard, and regards the FitzLeons as former tenants-in-chief of the de Lacy lordship. From the present day town square of Summerhill in County Meath, visitors can clearly make out the hill where the remains of Lynch Castle still stand, outlasting the formerly magnificent 19th century Summerhill House which was burned out in 1921 during the War of Independence. Hardiman, with his habit of mentioning variations on family histories, had also noted a variation on the story of Cnoc an Línsigh. In one version of the Lynch origins that is relegated to the footnotes, Hardiman says the first Lynch to arrive in Ireland was Andrew de Lynch, who was granted lands in Castleknock in Dublin. In this instance, Hardiman's source probably confused Castleknock in Dublin with Knock Castle in Meath, which was also known as Cnoc an Línsigh. This footnote goes on to say that John, the youngest son of Andrew de Lynch was the first Lynch to arrive in Galway in 1261.

Aside from the mystery of the first Lynch in Galway, we're faced with a more pertinent question: Who brought the Lynch name west to Galway from the rich agricultural lands in Co. Meath, and why? It's very likely that the family's relationship with the De Burgos opened the route to Galway. In a grant made around 1191, Leonisius de Bromiard names his son Thomas as his heir, but Thomas may have died as his place is subsequently taken by John Fitz Leon who begins to appear as heir to Leonisius in documents dated to 1212, followed then by mentions of his son Thomas Fitz Leones in regard to charters of the De Lacy family.

During this period, we see the gradual transformation of the family name. Scholars regard Leonisius of Bromiard as the eponym of the Lynch family but it's worth noting here that in the early Irish records, the same person can appear under several different versions of the same name: John Fitz Leon appears variously as Johannis Filii Leonis, John Fitz Lyons and John de Lynch, while Thomas Fitz Leon appears as Thomas Fitz Leones, Thomas Fitz Lyons or Thomas de Linche.

It's likely that John Fitz Leon's son Thomas became an in-law of the de Lacy family through Joan Fitz Leon, who married Simon de Geneville of the De Lacy family. By extension, Thomas became a relative of the de Burghs, as members of the de Burgh and de Lacy family intermarried. (It's often mentioned in older histories of the Lynch family that the clan descended from the de Lacy family or from William de Petit, although it's now clear that the early Anglo-Norman Lynches in fact married into these families, rather than descended from them.) Through their relationships with the de Lacy and de Burgh families, the Fitz Leons were well placed to take advantage of the opportunities in as-yet unconquered Connaught. So, in the century following their establishment in Meath, the Fitz Leons began to move west, towards Galway, along with a number of the other Anglo–Norman families.

King John granted Connaught to William de Burgh, who never gained control of the province, and William's son Richard Mór de Burgh took the conquest of Connaught upon himself, beginning around 1230 when he engaged in his first skirmishes with the Gaelic Irish, who were in no mind to allow De Burgh to gain control of their land. After unsuccessfully laying siege to the town of Galway in

1230, De Burgh gained control of the town in 1232. It's a matter of speculation, but it's quite likely that the Fitz Leons joined de Burgh's fighting forces. If De Burgh was assisted by Thomas de Linche, son of John Fitz Leon, and grandson of Leonisius de Bromiarde, then it makes sense that Thomas de Linche was granted an important position in the new administration.

As Earls of Ulster, the de Burghs enjoyed the right to appoint the sovereign or provost of Galway, and it was in 1274, according to Lynch family records, that Thomas de Linche became the first provost of Galway, with William De Lench listed as the collector of customs in the town in 1277. Thus began a period lasting several centuries during which the Lynch family became merchant princes and one of the wealthiest families in the land.

During the late 13th and early 14th century, the records of the Lynch family are derived chiefly from the family's own records, and Paul McNulty has compiled an extensive list of the family pedigrees in his book *Genealogy of the Anglo–Norman Lynches*. Records of Galway family histories drawn from the National Library of Ireland suggest that provost Thomas De Lench or De Lynch had two sons, James and William, who were the forebears of most of the Galway Lynch clans. These records suggest that William Lynch's grandson James was alive around the year 1400, and his grandson Edmund was on the way to becoming one of the first great wine merchants of Galway.

Readers may have noted the fact that the Gaelic name of Lynch appeared in the *Great Book of Genealogies* in the years leading up to 1165, while the first 'English' Lynches arrived to Ireland after 1169. For those keen to trace our ancestors back into the misty past, it sometimes proves irresistible to trace the merchant Lynches back to the times of the Norman conquest, and then shift the trail to the ancient Irish pedigrees, which stretch back from the 1160s all the way to the Milesian kings and thence to the times of Noah.

EAMONN A TUAN: WINE MASTER

The port town of Galway was well positioned for trade. With a vast hinterland where Gaelic and Anglo–Irish lords had huge herds of cattle, the Galway merchants had access to beef, butter, wool and hides, and quality Irish goods were in demand far beyond the island. Records from the town of Pisa indicate the arrival of 34,000 Irish hides in 1466–7 to supply the town's leather industry. The Atlantic coast off Galway was rich in cod, hake and herring, and boats from as far south as Portugal and Spain sailed into Irish waters in the summer laden with salt and returned at the end of summer heavy with salted fish.

Trade connected Galway merchants to other merchants up and down the Atlantic coast. Goods sought after in Ireland consisted mainly of wine, salt and spices, metal goods and good quality cloth. Cloth came from England but southern Europe became a significant source of trade. Salt was readily available in southern Europe, and Spain and Portugal became new sources of wine, replacing the traditional trade with Bordeaux which suffered during the wars between England and France.

Bristol in particular was an important link for Galway merchants. The towns had long been linked by trade. From the late 14th century, the Bristol merchant Richard Payns leased the Galway salmon fisheries, cornering the market for a while, and by the late 15th century, Galway was supplying up to one third of the imports into Bristol. Bristol, in turn, was a gathering place for merchants and seafarers from as far south as the Arab lands of northern Africa and as far north as Norway, and in Bristol, merchants swapped stories of new routes and opportunities. Sometimes they were more tight-lipped, as seafarers sought out new fishing grounds: the knowledge of these new grounds was zealously guarded. Ships from Bristol sailed as far north as Iceland in search of fish, and to bring provisions, and returned with tales of new lands to the west. With these extensive links, and their ability to fill ships with beef, hides and butter on outward journeys, and salt, wine and spices on the return journey, successful Galway merchants could earn themselves significant riches.

It's certain that wine was a major source of wealth for the Galway merchants, and the Lynches were the earliest and biggest players in this trade, reaching a commanding position by the early 15th century. Although contemporary histories of the wine trade into Ireland tend to associate the trade with the demand for wine produced by the sacraments of the Catholic Church, it's entirely likely that the wine trade reaches back to the pre-Christian era. Looking back over the great sweep of mercantile activity, it's clear that smart merchants looked for one particular commodity: that which kept customers coming back for more. More often than not, this involved addictive substances. The early wine trade produced great fortunes. A second wave of enormous wealth was generated by the sugar trade; the coffee and tobacco trade also proved hugely profitable.

Edmund Lynch was a pioneer in the Irish wine trade. Edmund, according to the Blake family records, was the great-great-grandson of William Lynch, and was sovereign of the town in 1434 and 1443. Edmund was also known as Eamonn A Tuan Lynch, apparently earning his name from the vast quantities of wine that he imported. (A 'tun' was a large barrel of wine holding 252 English gallons, and upwards of a thousand were imported into Galway each year.) It was Edmund who paid for and built the first bridge over the river Corrib in 1442. Eamonn A Tuan Lynch died in 1462; his son Thomas became Sovereign of Galway in 1476, but it was another Lynch of Galway, Germyn, who would gain a greater degree of fame through his moneymaking and seafaring schemes.

GERMYN LYNCH: MINT MAKER

Goldsmith, moneymaker, mint master, tour operator and merchant: Germyn Lynch (aka Germanus Lynch) was an ambitious Irish merchant prince who started out as the Irish mint master and spent the later part of his life travelling up and down the Atlantic from Iceland to Portugal.

Incredibly, Germyn Lynch was dismissed from the lucrative position of mint master four times, and subsequently reinstated each time before his fifth and final dismissal in 1483. Indeed, the recorded history of Germyn Lynch regards him as something of a scoundrel who abused his position. Yet, when we look a bit more closely at the era in which he operated, we see that the minting of coins was not only a craft but a political minefield. In the modern era, it's widely accepted that currencies should not be lightly changed or altered. The major changes in Ireland's currency in recent decades are decimalisation (1971) and converting from the Irish pound to the Euro (2001), yet both of these changes were extensively discussed and flagged, while still having their share of unforeseen consequences. During Lynch's reign as mint master, regulations changed several times each decade. The physical composition of coins changed several times, and King Edward IV ordered coins to be devalued a number of times. On top of that, wealthy merchants and landowners in Ireland and England pressured the authorities to change weights and designs to suit their own needs. In the midst of this numismatic chaos, Germyn Lynch laboured to keep up with his duties. At least one question remains unanswered: Did Germyn Lynch used the opportunity to earn illegitimate money for himself on the side?

We first come across the name of Germyn Lynch in the records of the then 100-year old Worshipful Company of Goldsmiths, when the young Germyn Lynch arrived in London in 1441 to begin an apprenticeship as a goldsmith. This wasn't a typical move for a young Irishman, so we can deduce that Germyn's family were not unfamiliar with the opportunities afforded to young craftsmen in London. We don't know where Lynch was born and it's possible that Germyn was either one of the Lynches of Galway, or one of the Lynches of Cnoc an Línsigh near Trim, ancestors of the Galway Lynches. (We do know that he owned a house and land in Galway that he was cheated out of by double-crossing merchants, but that doesn't prove his origins and he may have inherited the house or bought it.) Oddly enough, we know little of Germyn from the Galway Lynch family records, which does make it possible that Germyn was raised on the east coast.

Although Germyn Lynch lived seven centuries ago, we find his name appearing in diverse historical records ranging from legal records in Ireland to company records in London and port books in Bristol. In 1441, Lynch was admitted as an apprentice to the Worshipful Company of Goldsmiths as a 'Dutchman' (i.e. a foreigner), paying two shillings for the privilege. In 1446, five years after arriving in London, Germyn paid £4 13s 4d and was admitted to the freedom and liberty of the goldsmiths of London, giving him the right to work as a freeman. He spent the next decade in London, where he developed his business and took on apprentices, and by 1457 he was established as a citizen and goldsmith of standing. The chaos about to erupt in Ireland's financial realm would soon provide him with a new opportunity.

The monetary supply in Lynch's homeland was in disorder. The country suffered a shortage of silver coins, and old pennies and halfpennies from the 14th century were still in circulation. Illegal mints operated in several towns and the country was plagued by the circulation of forged money. Yet it was political rather than monetary policy that provided the impetus for change.

In 1459, in return for the support of Irish nobility for his campaign to gain the English crown, Richard Duke of York granted permission for Irish authorities to strike silver groats (normally equivalent to four pennies) at a lower weight than the English groat, and agreed to fix a mint at Trim Castle along with the Dublin mint. For the previous 250 years, since 1210, the weight of Irish coin had been fixed to an English standard, but the new standard was set at 45 grains of silver per groat as against 60 grains of silver per groat in England. (A troy ounce is 480 grains.) The benefit to Irish authorities of this divergence in weight was that it discouraged overseas landowners from repatriating the Irish coin back to England, for the new Irish coin would be only worth the equivalent of 3 pennies. Richard's plan was soon thrown into chaos. He died in battle in 1460, and his son Edward took the throne as Edward IV. A merchant called Thomas Barby had been appointed as keeper of the Irish mint in 1460: Germyn Lynch was appointed as master of the mint at Trim Castle in 1461. By 1463, Edward IV had appointed Lynch as warden and master of the Irish mint: "We grant power to the said Germyn to make all manner of ponsons, screws, graves and other instruments necessary to the said minters at London, or elsewhere...." Lynch would earn ten marks for making the mints, and was granted power to install labourers at his mint on punishment of imprisonment if they refused.

The warden was technically superior to the master of the mint, though Lynch held both positions. Although subordinate, the master's position was more lucrative, as the master could earn money directly from the minting process and through his subcontractors, and the master of the mint was a lifetime appointment. (In the UK, the position of master of the mint was replaced in 1870 by the Chancellor of the Exchequer). It's likely that the phrase 'he made a mint', meaning 'he made a large sum of money', has its origins in the practice of manufacturing the moneymaking equipment itself. On his appointment, Lynch began to manufacture the punches and dies necessary to mint coins, starting in Dublin and Waterford. It took until 1463 before Lynch's patent was widely recognised, and he was granted the right to coin money in Dublin, Trim, Galway, Waterford, Limerick, Carlingford and Drogheda. He almost immediately faced a complex set of challenges and during his lifetime as mint master the English administration frequently changed the weights and designs of Irish coins in the course of an ongoing struggle between English and Irish authorities. During the 1460s and 1470s, the Irish mint was required to produce sets of coins of different weights and designs so diverse that modern students of coins are still trying to make sense of the surviving varieties.

The mint master's pay came from the minting process itself. Lynch's original instructions regarding the production of groats required him to produce 120 fourpenny pieces per ounce troy of silver, and he was allowed to keep five of these pieces for himself. There were ways for a skilled moneymaker to increase his profits, for the laws allowed a slight variation in weight above or below the standard. Researchers have found that several of Lynch's 45 grain groats weighted 44.5 grains, and as a half-grain loss of weight fell within the legal limits, the regular production of marginally underweight coins could add up to a healthy profit for Lynch when maintained over time.

Quite apart from Lynch's sleight of hand, the laws governing money were convoluted due to the regularly changing political situation. In 1464, King Edward IV ordered that the English standard groat be lowered to 48 grains. He ordered Germyn Lynch to cease using his own equipment and directed that coins be minted only with equipment produced by the Tower of London. The reduction of the weight in the English coin to 48 grains brought the English coin very close to the Irish standard of 45 grains, and it seems that Lynch subsequently began striking Irish coins of about 41 grains to maintain the advantage. (Some historians of money have suggested that Lynch was taking advantage of the rather obscure difference between the 'Tower Ounce' of 450 grains and the 'Troy Ounce' of 480 grains. In this way he was able to legitimately claim that he was sticking diligently to an 'ounce'.)

In 1465, merely one year after lowering the weight of coins, Edward decided to introduce a new design, solely with an English imprint. This inadvertently introduced a new problem as new Irish coins now shared the imprint of the 48 grain English groat, and looked identical, but were of a lighter 41 grain weight. From 1465 to 1467 Germyn Lynch was kept busy minting the new coins.

As the new Irish and English coins had identical designs, few people were able to differentiate between the heavier English and lighter Irish coin. As a result, the coins poured out of Ireland into England, resulting in severe economic hardship for Ireland. The 'new' Irish coin began to circulate in England at par with the English coins, further upsetting English merchants who petitioned the King to give the Irish coin a distinctive design, setting in store another financial calamity.

In 1467, the king appointed Sir John Tiptoff as his new judiciar for Ireland, and Tiptoff immediately moved to reintroduce specifically Irish coins. His plan was to create a new very light groat (of 22.5 grains) and a double groat of 45 grains. To generate the new coins, Tiptoff made all previous coins illegal, requiring that all people holding silver coin returned them to the mint to be recast into distinctively 'Irish' coins. Tiptoff's plan had at least two unintended consequences. It all but guaranteed that the economy would grind to a halt with no coin in circulation. Also, locals unsurprisingly failed to rush to the mint, where they would lose about 40% of the value of their coins, and instead hastened to get their money to England, resulting in an additional outflow of capital to England that only exacerbated the dire economic situation.

As mint master, Lynch was at the mercy of a continual struggle between Irish authorities who tried to maintain their coinage at a lower weight than English coins, and English authorities trying to impose control on Irish coinage that often ended up circulating in England at a lower weight. Yet Lynch proved adept at exploiting the rapidly-evolving dynamic between the two countries. Modern numismatists have shown that Lynch was already wise to ways to exploit legal loopholes to shave tiny profits for himself one coin at at time. Did he cross the line into illegal activity?

We come across the first charges of fraudulent behaviour against Lynch when was charged with producing underweight coin in Drogheda in 1472. Although directed to produce 44 shillings per pound of bullion, Lynch was charged with producing 48 shillings per pound and keeping four for himself. As a result of the charges, he was removed from his position.

There are no records of the case itself, but it's worth noting that Lynch was not the only minter of coin in Ireland, even though he was warden and master of the mint, so it is possible that another minter was producing underweight coins. He was pardoned by the king and reinstated to his position in 1473, but all coins were directed to be minted in Dublin Castle, with the other mints losing their moneymaking privileges, at least for a number of years.

Many coins struck after 1473 have a distinctive 'G' printed on the coin, thought to be a mark introduced by Germyn Lynch to distinguish his own coin, and numismatists found that these coins are of remarkable consistency. Despite Lynch's apparently newfound eagerness to distinguish his work, English merchants brought another charge against him in 1474 and he was once again dismissed.

Around this time, Lynch decided to return to the more traditional work of his family, and began a second career as a merchant and seafarer that was interspersed with returns to and dismissals from the mint. Lynch quickly discovered that the mercantile world was full of sharp practices. An incident recorded in England in 1474 suggests that Lynch was successfully double–crossed by fellow merchants who may have been aware of his disgraced position as a goldsmith. In that year, Lynch began his merchant career by taking a cargo of wine from Portugal to Ireland. Having damaged a mast along the way, he took his ship *Mary Leybourne* into Kinsale to fix the mast and retrofit the ship for a planned voyage to Spain. The year 1475 was a 'Holy Year', during which pilgrims to the shrine of St. James de Compostela were granted full remission from temporal sins, and there was tremendous demand for passage to Spain in these Holy Years.

In need of a loan to do the repairs, Lynch dispatched his servant Esmond Terger to Limerick to arrange a loan from the merchants Walter White and Gerot Lewes. Terger duly arranged a loan of almost £25 with arrangements for the repayment to be made through Bruges or London. Three Galway merchants, John Ffrench, James Fitzwilliam Blake and Thomas Blake, who may have been banking on Lynch's newfound infamy as a cheat, conspired with Terger, White and Lewes to outwit Lynch.

White and Lewes took a case to the Galway Sovereign Thomas Fitzsaundre Lynch, claiming that they had not been repaid, although Germyn Lynch rejected the claim and maintained that he had repaid the loan through London as arranged. The Sovereign found against his namesake, awarding Germyn Lynch's Galway house and land to the merchants. Lynch sought redress by having the wrongdoers arraigned before the King's representatives, but as far as we know, they never appeared. (The incident shows that the Lynch family in Galway did not necessarily display favouritism towards their own; the

Sovereign was the son of Eamonn A Tuan Lynch of the previous chapter, and was possibly unimpressed by Germyn's entry into the wine trade.)

With his southern ventures wracked by this dispute, Lynch then turned to northern parts. Galway was an important stopping point for Bristol ships bound for Iceland, and Lynch decided to work the Bristol-Galway-Iceland route. Records from the Bristol port books show Lynch departing Bristol as master of the ship *John Evangelist* in March 1478, bound for Iceland with a consignment of goods being shipped by John Pynke of Bristol. The rich fishing grounds off Iceland were attracting fleets of ships from England and the Baltic sea, so demand was high for provisions, and for salt to cure the fish. *John Evangelist* carried flour, 10 tons of salt, 9 barrels of butter and lengths of cloth valued at £5 16s 8d. The trip to Iceland in the springtime was a profitable but dangerous venture, and demanded no little skill of the shipmaster, but Lynch successfully pulled off the trip.

On his return from Iceland, Lynch found himself once again reinstated to his position of master of the mint, sharing the position with London goldsmith William Hatecliff, but once again his position was challenged and he faced two furthers dismissals and reappointments in 1478-9 and 1480. As before, during these periods of dismissal, Lynch occupied himself as a merchant. Lynch's ship *Michael* carried herring, salmon and hides from Ireland to Bristol, and his final appearance in the Bristol port books was in March of 1480 when he left the port with a cargo of salt, honey, alum and "old corrupt wine." (Laws prohibited the sale of old or corrupt wines in England, and it was used instead for picking of fish such as herring or in the curing of hides, or imported to Ireland where it could be mixed with good wine.)

Richard III took the crown in 1483, and installed a new master of the mint. The patent letters and acts of Germyn Lynch were made void and he was "cast out of his place" for the final time. The date and place of his death are unknown: his house and land in Galway were already in the hands of his adversaries.

Recalling Lynch's world of bankers, merchants and magnates, and his travels along the Atlantic coast, the historian Timothy O'Neill observed that even the few surviving records of Germyn Lynch hint at a life of adventure. The full life history of Germyn Lynch, wrote O'Neill, "would surely equal the most exciting imaginings of any writer of historical novels".

THE MERCHANTS OF GALWAY

Galway is known as the City of the Tribes, named for the 14 families that dominated the commerce and administration of the town for several hundred years, although the 14 tribes families did not arrive together en masse. The first of the families arrived in the 13th century included the Anglo–Norman families Athy, Blake, Bodkin, Joyce, Lynch, Martin and Skerrett. Along with the De Burgh family, these wealthy Norman families set about fortifying the town, establishing it as an Anglo-Norman stronghold in Connaught and a trading port that would eventually allow these families to become international merchants.

Over the course of the 14th and 15th centuries these families were joined by the D'Arcy, Browne, Ffrench and Morris families, also of Norman or Anglo-Norman origin, and the Kirwans, who alone among the tribe families claimed Irish origins. During the years between the incorporation of the town in 1484 and the arrival of Cromwell in 1654 and subsequent change in the town's laws disqualifying Catholics from the Mayoralty, the 14 families controlled the trade of the town and dominated the administration.

The charges brought against Germyn Lynch by a sovereign of the same surname suggests that there was a degree of independent justice in the town, but in general the tribe families married their sons and daughters to one another and operated like merchant princes. The tribes considered themselves to be Englishmen, and made every effort to distinguish themselves from the Irish inhabitants of the surrounding countryside.

Yet two forces limited the power of the tribes. In matters of religion, the town of Galway had traditionally belonged to the diocese of Annaghdown, although Annaghdown had then been united with the archdiocese of Tuam in the 14th century. The tribes also chafed at the control enjoyed by the de Burgh family, who controlled the appointment of the Provost or Sovereign of the town. In 1484 the tribe families moved to throw off these restrictions and there's little doubt that tribe families acted with singular unity of purpose in this regard.

They petitioned the Archbishop of Tuam to release them from the jurisdiction of Annaghdown, and enable them to have their own jurisdiction under the Church of St. Nicholas, and also sent a petition to Pope Innocent VIII, presenting themselves as "modest and civil", surrounded by the savage Irish who were given to robbing and killing the good townspeople of Galway. The Archbishop, wary of the power of the tribes, agreed to raise the Church of St. Nicholas into a collegiate, with the power to elects its own warden and vicars. Pope Innocent VIII agreed to confirmation of the petition.

It's a measure of the confidence of the tribes that they simultaneously moved to gain control over the administration of the town. In the same year, they petitioned King Richard III for a new charter that would allow them to directly elect their own mayors and bailiffs. King Richard III agreed to grant the town a new charter, which also removed all power from the Clanricard de Burghs. Under the new charter, the town would elect its own mayors and bailiffs and no person could enter the town without license. In one fell swoop, the tribes had gained themselves control of a virtual city-state.

Pierce Lynch Fitz John was elected as the first mayor in 1485, and the mayorship remained the exclusive preserve of the tribe families for the next 169 years, although the Lynch family were first among equals. From 1485 to 1654, 80 mayors came from the Lynch family with no other family supplying more than 20 mayors. The tribe families exercised almost total control over commerce and the town's administration. It was, significantly, a period during which the Spanish empire conquered the Americas, and opened up massive new commercial opportunities for the merchants of Galway.

Enjoying such power, the tribes were keen to present themselves as upstanding citizens worthy of the independence granted them by church and state. No family had as much at stake as the Lynches. Their influence and standing in the wine trade had raised the family to fabulous riches, and they had spent some of that wealth on bridges and churches. As giants of the wine trade, the Lynches enjoyed a commercial relationship with the churches, who required a constant supply for both religious and non-religious purposes. With this standing, there was wisdom in maintaining good public relations, and it's perhaps more than coincidence that the most famous Lynch legend is dated to 1493, a few years after the family gained an unrivalled position of power in Galway.

THE MAYOR OF GALWAY

When John Ford and John Wayne made *The Man Who Shot Liberty Valence*, critics noted that it was Ford's way of acknowledging the role he had played in mythologizing the American west. Ford also played a small role in mythologizing the Irish West, in *The Quiet Man*, but his frontier Westerns continued to resonate with the American public through the Reagan era and even into the new millenium. A famous line about fact and legend is delivered at the end of the movie, after Senator Ramson Stoddard (James Stewart) has recounted to a newspaperman for the first time the true story of how he came to be known as the man who shot the bully Liberty Valence. He explains that it was Tom Doniphon (played by John Wayne) who had really killed Valence, and Doniphon had allowed Stoddard to take the credit for it, considering Stoddard to be a decent, upstanding man who should go to Washington to fight against corruption. Upon finishing the tale, Stoddard asks the newspaperman if he will print the story, but the journalist instead rips up his notes, acknowledging that the public, rightly or wrongly, preferred salutary legends over mere fact. "This is the West, sir," he says solemnly: "When the legend becomes fact, print the legend."

The story of the 15th century Mayor Lynch of Galway who hanged his only son is one of the most famous tales of Galway, and although the story is almost certainly fabricated, it still takes pride of place in tourist guides. The job of the historian is to separate fact from mythology and legend. The "truth" is often more mundane and boring than the legend, and doesn't sell as well, but sometimes the truth is more remarkable than the legend. Such is the tension between legend and fact: the merchants and administrators of Galway believe that tourists, a major source of revenue for the town, come to Galway for the legends, not the facts. The legend also serves as something of an origin myth for the Galway of the Tribes, upstanding and unbending in their administration of justice, far as though that may have been from the truth.

The story of Mayor Lynch dates from 1493 and has survived and even grown through the centuries, appearing widely in tourist guidebooks and in literature from the early 19th century. In the mid-19th century, when the new railway line brought tourists to Galway, the city authorities built a monument to commemorate the episode, and the "Lynch Window" on Market Street with its placard and skull and crossbones is now a famous tourist attraction in its own right. (Some historians have even suggested that the concept of 'Lynching' originated with Mayor Lynch and his son.) The story of Mayor Lynch is almost certainly a legend, but like many great legends, it's based on elements of truth and real persons.

When the tribes of Galway moved to gain control of the town in 1484, the town's new charter gave the townspeople the right to nominate their own mayor. Seven of the first eight mayors of Galway came from the Lynch family. The ninth mayor, James Lynch Fitz Stephen, became the most famous.

Almost every modern version of the story can be traced back to James Hardiman's *History of the Town and County of Galway*, and Hardiman's version of the story can be traced back to a single manuscript from the late 17th century, which had already gone missing by the time Hardiman wrote his story. The monument now standing in Galway city was probably nothing to do with the story itself, but over the centuries, it became the physical manifestation of the story, and took on a life of its own. How did this all happen?

James Hardiman was a trained lawyer from a wealthy Mayo family, and his first publication *History of the Town and County of Galway* in 1820 was a bestseller in its time and was regarded as the standard history of Galway for many years. Although Hardiman aimed for historical accuracy, he was surely aiming at some degree of commercial success for his publication, and the Mayor of Galway story added a large slice of entertainment value to his narrative.

Hardiman's account of the story of Mayor Lynch begins by mentioning that the Pope and the King allowed the incorporation of Galway to proceed due to "the unsullied honour of the inhabitants, whose strict adherence to truth and love of impartial justice became universally proverbial". The proof of this love of justice, says Hardiman, is illustrated by a single story, "an appalling instance of inflexible virtue … which stands paralleled by very few examples in the history of mankind". In a footnote, Hardiman writes that many of the minor incidents described in the story may be fanciful, but do nothing to affect the truth of the main occurrence in the story. He adds that his version of the story had been drawn from an account titled "George the third" by the Reverend Edward Mangin, and extended with some extra details. While admitting that there are also variations on the story, "few transactions of so old a date stand better authenticated than that concerning young Lynch". Indeed, Hardiman added, he had personally seen several ancient manuscripts recording the incident.

Hardiman tells the story of James Lynch Fitzstephens, an "opulent merchant" and mayor, who travelled to Spain to conduct trade in the city of Cadiz with a merchant called Gomez. To pay back the reception afforded to him by Gomez, the mayor offered to bring to Galway the son of the Spanish merchant, to allow him to see something of the world. Walter, the mayor's son, was one of "the finest youths of his time", whose good looks, fine manners and physical height and strength endeared him to the people of Galway.

This abundance of gifts encouraged the young man to libertinism to the dismay of his purity-loving father, who hoped that young Gomez would have a good influence on his son. Walter was in love with a woman called Agnes Blake. One evening, in the company of Agnes and Gomez, Walter began to suspect that Agnes was becoming interested in the young Gomez. He upbraided Agnes, and the evening ended badly. The following evening, passing by Agnes's residence, Walter saw the young Spaniard coming out of the house. Agnes's father, fluent in Spanish, had invited the young Gomez but Walter suspected that the Spaniard and Agnes were continuing their affair. He chased the young Spaniard towards the docks, stabbed him in the heart, and threw the body into the water. He then fled into the nearby woods.

The next morning, the sea returned the Spaniard's body to shore, and a group of men led by the Mayor set out to find the guilty party. They soon came upon Walter, who had been beset by guilt and was returning from the woods to confess his crime. The horrified Mayor took his son into custody, and led him towards the prison, through crowds of shocked locals who had turned out to find out what all the fuss was about. "Within the short compass of a few days," wrote Hardiman, "a small town in the West of Ireland, with a population, at the time, of little more than three thousand persons, beheld a sight of which but one or two similar examples occur in the entire history of mankind – a father sitting in judgment, like another Lucius Junius Brutus, on his only son, and, like him too, condemning that son to die, as a sacrifice to public justice." A short trial followed, brought to a swift conclusion by the confession of the murderer, and Walter was returned to prison, which lay right next to the Mayor's house. Crowds surrounded the prison, at first expressing murmurs of regret, but eventually becoming rowdy and tumultuous, and determined not to see the young man condemned to death. In his prison cell, Walter began to wonder at his own madness. With some hints that compassion would be extended to the prisoner, the crowds were induced to disperse. The unyielding mayor descended to the prison dungeon, and informed his son that the execution would proceed on course the following morning. With a priest in attendance (whom according to Hardiman was the source of this story), the Mayor prayed for the soul of his son, and remained together with his son through the "woeful" night.

The boy's mother and his relatives pleaded with the Mayor to change his mind. The crowds returned, and pushed ever closer to the house. The soldiers, overcome by the passion of the crowd and the family, retreated from their duties. Yet the Mayor would not be swayed:

'It is probable he was prepared for this extremity; for turning back, and still keeping hold of his son, he mounted by a winding stairs within the building, which led to an arched window that overlooked the street in which the populace was assembled: he there presented himself and his victim, about whose neck he had previously fastened the rope with which he had been bound, and, securing the other end in an iron projecting from the wall, "You have little time to live, my son" said he; "let the care of your soul employ these few moments – take the last embrace of your unhappy father:" – he embraced his unfortunate son, and launched him into eternity! A few moments put an end to his existence.'

Expecting instant death from the fury of the rabble below, the father stood and waited, but this act of greatness awed the crowd, who stood still in amazement for a time, and then slowly melted away. Poor Agnes, according to Hardiman's account, died of grief and the Mayor himself was never seen in public again.

'His house still exists in Lombard Street, which is yet known by the name of "Dead Man's Lane;" and the execution is said to have taken place at a window in the rear of the house; although the vulgar error is, that he was suspended over the front window, which is distinguished by a handsome representation, carved in black marble, of a skull, with two bones crossed underneath. It is dated in 1624; and is supposed to have been put up by some of the family as a public memorial of a transaction which succeeding times looked up on with astonishment and which the production of the arts in this country should perpetuate with statues.'

Hardiman's story, replete with jealous sons, foreign merchant princes, murder, hubris and intransigent justice, is Shakespearean in its sweep, and in the years following its publication, the Mayor of Galway story propagated throughout the kingdom. One of the first mentions of the story was in 1830, when John McGregor repeated (and validated) Hardiman's story in *True Stories from the Histories of Ireland*.

Travel writers couldn't resist Hardiman's tale. The 1820s and 1830s witnessed the advent of the modern travel guide, among them Prince Hermann von Pückler-Muskau's *Tour in England, Ireland and France in the years 1826, 1827, 1828 and 1829: With Remarks on the Manners and Customs of the Inhabitants, and Anecdotes of Distinguished Public Characters*. On his travels, the Prince had spent time in Galway and recounted at length the story of the Mayor of Galway, which he claimed to have picked up from "fragments of a local Chronicle" that he spied in a grocer's shop while inquiring about the black marble plaque with its skull and crossbones that he had seen earlier in the day. He then proceeded to re-tell the Hardiman tale, without attribution.

The prince published his book in Germany, where it became a success: the book was subsequently translated for the English market and published there in 1832. The Prince's tales were eagerly awaited to the extent that the *London Literary Gazette* published two extracts from the book in November 1831, including the Prince's tale of the Mayor of Galway.

At this point, the Rev. Mangin re-enters the story. In a wonderful piece of research in the 1969 issue of the Galway Journal of Historical and Archaeological Research, James Mitchell traced the progress of the Reverend Mangin's "luckless legend" onto the pages of Hardiman's history of Galway and from there to widespread fame. Having observed his story from George the third appearing first in McGregor's True Stories and then in von Pückler-Muskau's tales, the Reverend was moved to write a letter to the Sun newspaper, outlining the comic progress of his "redoubted fiction", and begging the editor for an opportunity to set the story straight. As the Rev. Mangin wrote to a friend, Dr. Tierney, of Hardiman's account: "I invented the story of the heroic Mayor of Galway, founding it on a few traditionary incidents ... and tho' exceedingly proud of the compliment paid to me, am sorry he has introduced such a trifling incident into his very able work, in which, in history as it should be, every other part is written in the purest spirit of truth. It is still, however, a matter of triumph for me to have my name mingled with the history of a town and people I am and ever shall be attached to."

While Rev. Mangin awaited a reply from the Sun's editor, he noted yet another variation of the fable when a play opened in Dublin titled 'The Warden of Galway'. The play was based on a different version of the Mayor of Galway story, where the Mayor's son goes to Galway and murders a Spaniard on the return journey. At that stage, Mangin may have realised that he would not easily divert such a compelling tale. Travel writers sought out the evidence of this dastardly deed: In 1833, in Tour of Connemara, the Irish author Maria Edgeworth tells of seeing with her own eyes the "black marble marrowbones and death's head inscription, with the date 1493 still on the walls".

With the Mayor of Galway story now taking on a life of its own and appearing in a number of guides, the skull and crossbones on Lombard Street took on monumental significance, although there was no indication that it had anything whatsoever to do with the

Mayor of Galway story, particularly as it was dated from 1624, 130 years after the alleged incident. Nonetheless, story after story was writing the skull and crossbones into the story of the execution.

By 1844, the house on Lombard Street (now Market Street) was beginning to crumble. The town commissioners ordered the demolition of the building, compensated the owner, and saved the skull and bones which was dispatched to Dublin for safekeeping. Conscious of the growing fame of the Lynch legend and its material representation in the skull and bones, the Town Commissioners met to establish a "Committee for the Re-Erection of the Cross Bones" in early 1845, though this process was held up for several years by the arrival of the great famine.

By 1846, Hardiman himself had begun to suspect that the power of the story lay more in its myth than fact. Other respected historians such as Hely Dutton had suggested that the story had no historical origin, and Hardiman came to the conclusion that he had over-egged the story in his original account. However, Hardiman's change of mind had little or no impact on the wider public. Once the famine had passed, the Town Commissioners met once again to consider the fate of the monument. With funds low, and other priorities at hand, the committee moved slowly and the skull and bones languished in Dublin. In 1851 the railway line from Dublin to Galway was completed, and the Town Commissioners began to fret that the town's most famous monument had not yet been restored to a public place.

The newspaper *Warden of Galway* urged the town's commissioners to proceed at speed, while simultaneously cementing the myth into place: "Some years ago, the Corporation, in the prosecution of their bad taste, destroyed the house where the tragic event occurred, which was the principal object of attraction to every traveller that visits Galway, and ever since, these interesting memorials have been cast into an obscure corner of the Gas House, much to the disappointment of every Western tourist." By 1855, the Commissioners finally raised the funds for a new memorial that would incorporate the skull and bones, set into a wall below a stone window frame suggestive of the original window where the execution had taken place. The new memorial was erected on Lombard Street by the side of the Church of St. Nicholas, with an accompanying tablet that read:

'This ancient memorial of the stern and unbending justice of the chief magistrate of this city James Lynch Fitzstephen elected Mayor ad 1493 who condemned and executed his own guilty son Walter on this spot has been restored to this its ancient site AD1854 with the approval of the town commissioners V Revd Peter Daly P.P. & Vicar of. St Nicholas.'

The monument, sitting awkwardly at the edge of the graveyard of the church, is a pastiche, and the combined effect of the stone window, the skull and bones memorial, and the commemorative tablet implied that the original execution had taken place at that very spot, from the stone window, and that the skull and bones was the original memorial itself. The monument to a story started to wind back on itself. A decade later, when William Wilde, wrote the travelogue *Lough Corrib*, he took his readers on a trip down William Street and then "on by the house where the skull and crossbones commemorates the story of the 'Warden of Galway'": Wilde's travel book directs readers to a fabricated monument commemorating a play loosely based on a written historical account that was itself based on a novel.

Over the years, the story continued to smuggle itself into the works of Ireland's great writers. James Joyce used the name Lynch for one of his characters, and according to James Joyce's biographer Richard Ellmann, Joyce decided to use the name because "Lynch as mayor of Galway had hanged his own son, and in *Ulysses* he shows Lynch leaving Stephen in the lurch". James Joyce also wrote about the Lynch story for a Trieste newspaper, incorporating the story of Mayor Lynch and adding some flourishes including the charming detail that the Church of St. Nicholas still holds a letter sent from the Borgia Pope to accompany the rosary beads he had dispatched to this man of honour. (The rosary beads belonged to legend, as did Joyce's letter.) Joyce also places Lynch's residence as "the dark and gloomy castle that still shadows the main street" (Lynch's castle), adding yet another change of location.

While writing his research into this many-headed story in the 1960s, which he updated in the 1970s as contributors noted the various stories based on the original, James Mitchell drily noted rumours that producers were looking to turn the Mayor Lynch story into a film. (Forty years later, this still hasn't happened, though each act of re-telling the story seems to open up further possibilities.) Mitchell was acknowledging the power of the legend, for while his factual debunking of the story was being printed in a relatively obscure journal of local history, film producers and famous novelists were drawn inexorably to the legend.

Once Mitchell had traced the apparently unstoppable momentum of the Mayor Lynch 'tradition', a question remained: exactly how and where did the Mayor Lynch story originate? Hardiman claimed that his story was based not just on tradition but on several "ancient manuscripts" that had passed through his own hands. In 'Mayor Lynch of Galway', James Mitchell examined the provenance of these documents, and discovered that the various "ancient manuscripts" were based on a 'Collegiate MS' (manuscript) of unknown date, that had gone missing several centuries earlier. The original story, it appears, derived from an account recorded from this 'Collegiate MS' by a certain Fr. De Aroya of the Dominican Order, who came to Galway in 1674 to investigate the credentials of Dominick Lynch, who was under consideration for appointment as regent of the College of St. Thomas of Aquine in Seville in Spain.

In Galway, Fr. De Aroya received testimony of witnesses and was shown a Collegiate Manuscript from the archives of the order. Fr de Aroya took this collegiate manuscript back to Spain, and Dr. Lynch was duly confirmed in his new position. Almost twenty years later, in 1693, Dr. Lynch had a notary copy an extract of the manuscript, which he then sent back to Galway, possibly for the use of other family members who had moved to the West Indies and wanted to document their ancestry.

One copy of the document made its way to John Lynch Alexander of Galway, who would subsequently provide this manuscript to Hardiman as proof of the Mayor Lynch story. Yet in the original story, there is no mention of any Spaniard, which is odd given that Dr. Lynch was about to be appointed to a Spanish college: Details of a Spanish victim of murder might have compelled Fr. De Aroya to seek further information, as it would have showed the Lynch family ready to address any wrongs regardless of familial loyalties. Neither is there any mention in these accounts of the skull and crossbones plaque of 1624, despite Fr. De Aroya being taken on a tour of the town.

Mitchell also finds that the historian Rev. John Lynch (c. 1599 – c. 1677) makes no mention of the Mayor Lynch story, or of the alleged plaque of 1624. Neither does the historian Roderick O'Flaherty, who wrote *West or H–Iar Connaught* (which was finally published in 1846) and *Ogygia* (1684), mention the Mayor Lynch story. Neither did the story appear in the *Annals of the Kingdoms of Ireland*, compiled in the 1630s, or in a compilation of the town's municipal records by JT Gilbert. Mitchell comes to the conclusion – along with several other 20th century historians – that the Mayor Lynch story was an invention, albeit a clever and compelling invention.

The historians had their say but the merchants of Galway continued to honour the Mayor Lynch 'tradition', and the tourists continued to flock to 'Lynch's window'. In 1972, the *Connacht Tribune* wrote that the debunking of the Mayor Lynch story of 1493 did not weaken the case for preserving the Lynch window and the skull and crossbones: "The Mayor Lynch story of stern and unbending justice is intriguing in its own right, and coupled with the memorial in Lombard Street, is of substantial financial benefit to Galway. Every guide book of Galway tells the story ... The story brings people to Galway. It may well be that Galway people should know that the Lynch story has no foundation in fact but that is no reason why it should now be regarded as something to be expurgated from the guide books or that they should look with distaste on the Memorial Window. By all means retain that monument."

The 'Lynch Window' was once again restored and moved back a number of feet from the sidewalk in 1978, with Ireland's tourist board Brd Fáilte paying half the cost of restoration. Tourist guides continued – and continue – to fudge any cracks in the story, with some exceptions. In *Tourist Trails of Old Galway*, published in 1978, Prof. E. Rynne made note of the restored monument and duly re-told the story of Mayor Lynch. He concluded: "If [the Lynch window] really is a late-18th century invention, then one must surely congratulate the people of Galway for laying on a tourist trap so early!"

Incidentally, Mayor James Lynch's son Andrew did leave a record of his activities in Galway after his failed attempt to build a canal from Lough Atalia to Poulavourline; it was thereafter known as 'Lynch's folly'.

THE WINE LYNCHES

It's a distinguishing feature of the Galway tribes that they invested in trading commodities that had built-in demand, or kept consumers coming back for more: sugar, tobacco, salt, spices and wine were among their most popular products. Eventually, the merchants became producers of many of those products themselves, especially through their Caribbean and American plantations. On the European side, the merchants moved into the wholesale of wine, and the Lynch family were one of the few that became winegrowers. These days, the Lynch family are almost totally – but not entirely – absent from the wine business, although the family name survives in the trade.

Wine features heavily in the history of the Lynch family. From the 15th century onwards, we have stories of people such as Eamonn A Tuan, the merchant who imported wine in great quantities, and wine features also in the stories of 15th century merchant Germyn Lynch. In the legends of the late 15th century Mayor of Galway, the purchase of a cargo of Spanish wine is often the reason given for the Mayor's trip to Spain. Galway was a superior natural port to Dublin and the merchants built wine vaults in the town centre capable of storing thousands of barrels. The Galway merchants traded wine all the way to the east coast cities of Drogheda and Dublin.

Initially dealing with local merchant families along the Atlantic coast, the Galway tribes soon started following the practice of placing a family member as a local agent, all the better to note local trends

51

and prices. While some wine historians claim that the major shift to France and the continent happened when the merchant families followed King James II into exile in 1690s, the Galway merchant families of Bodkin, Blake, Ffrench and Lynch were by that time already well established in trading houses in the coastal towns of St. Malo, St. Rochelle, Roeun, Bordeaux, Lisbon, Cadiz and Malaga. The town of Bordeaux traded with several Irish ports, and even had a school for Irish students from the beginning of the 17th century.

Today, the name of Lynch-Bages is well known as one of the finer Bordeaux wines, and its story starts with the Galway merchant John Lynch. Born in 1669, he served as an officer in the Irish army and fought at the Battle of the Boyne. He left for France in 1691 following the defeat of the Jacobites in what is popularly remembered as the Flight of the Wild Geese. Lynch set himself up in business in Bordeaux as a wool and leather merchant, and prospered. In 1709 he married Guillemette Constant and the following year he was naturalised as a French citizen. They had three children, among them Thomas–Michel Lynch, who married Elizabeth Drouillard in 1740. Drouillard was heiress to the domaine close to the town of Pauillac, on the banks of the Gironde. Although only 12 kilometres square, the locality of Pauillac is also home to some of the finest French wines of Château Latour, Château Lafite-Rothschild and Château Mouton-Rothschild. The Douillard estate became known as Lynch-Bages. Jean-Baptiste Lynch, the eldest son of Thomas Lynch, fulfilled his father's ambitions to have a lawyer in the family, and was appointed by Louis XV as Counsellor to the Bordeaux Parliament. However, it wasn't a good time to be a wealthy landowner and Jean-Baptiste was imprisoned in 1793. He survived the revolution as once again took public office, continuing the family tradition by becoming the Mayor of Bordeaux.

Jean-Baptiste's parents had gifted him the Lynch-Bages estate on his marriage but he delegated the running of the estate to his brother

Michel. Neither man left an heir, but the name Lynch-Bages has remained in use until today. (It was the wine of choice for the higher level civil servants in Ireland at a time when everyone else was drinking Blue Nun or Black Tower.) While Lynch-Bages remains a world-renowned wine, the current owners of the Lynch-Bages estate, the Cazes family, developed another wine honouring the name of Michel Lynch, which is now easily found in Irish wine shops and supermarkets. Almost two hundred years after the end of the Lynch association with the estate, the name lives on and in recent years the estate has added the labels Echo de Lynch-Bages and Pauilla de Lynch-Bages.

These impressive brand names are a guarantee of quality. Right? Not entirely, as it turns out. In a 2001 study at the University of Bordeaux, a scientist served cheap wine to a group of oenology students. One batch of the wine was served in expensive bottles, and another was served the wine in cheap bottles. The students, tricked by the labels and by the power of expectation, duly pronounced the 'expensive' wine to be better.

So we come to the wonderfully named Kermit Lynch, who began importing wine from Europe to California in the 1970s. Lynch is a musician and writer along with being a wine retailer and importer and has shown an admirable streak of individuality in his 40 years in the wine business, disregarding the famous big estate wines in favour of small family estates that have stuck to time–honoured winemaking techniques. He's not just appreciated in California: Lynch was awarded the 'Legion d'Honneur' by the French government in 2005 for his devotion to wine culture. Starting into the wine business in 1972, Lynch's instincts led him to concentrate on Italian and French wines, following in the footsteps of the Galway Lynches by importing wines from Europe (though Kermit Lynch's destination was California rather than Galway). Travelling back and forth to Europe to select the wines himself, he observed the subtleties of how the wine was served (as in some estates, both red and white were served at cellar temperature) and began shipping the wine back to California in refrigerated containers to maintain its properties. Focusing on mostly small family-run estates, Lynch introduced many wines that were previously unfamiliar to American wine drinkers, writing prodigiously about each wine in an effort to educate his audience. (His 1988 book *Adventures On The Wine Route* has never been out of print.)

Lynch's labelling of wine bottles took an unusual twist when he objected to the introduction of health warnings on wine. As an importer, Lynch had to have his labels approved by the government but he was appalled at the claim that wine may be dangerous for people's health. He tried to soften the warning's impact by including quotes from the Bible: "Take a little wine for thy stomachs every day"; Louis Pasteur's observation that "wine is the most hygienic beverage known to man"; and Thomas Jefferson's observation that "A good wine is a necessity of life". The government was not impressed. After several years of persistence, Lynch was allowed to add his quotes. As both a player and fan of roots music, he has written and recorded several country music albums.

It would be remiss not to mention the Mutt Lynch Winery in Sonoma County, California. This Lynch family are dog lovers; their logo features a greyhound in place of the Lynx usually honoured on the traditional Lynch crest.

WESTWARD BOUND

There are more than 100,000 Lynches living in north America. It's one of the 250 most popular surnames in the country, and includes almost 10,000 Americans of African descent. While there was intermarriage between African-Americans and post-Famine Irish emigrants, it's likely that most black Lynches derived their names from the previous wave of Lynches who had access to money and became plantation owners, giving their names to their former slaves. How did the Lynch family spread so widely across America prior to the mid-18th century?

The answer lies in the spread of the merchant Lynches, beginning in the 17th century. There's no doubt that the Lynch family of that era were fabulously wealthy. Throughout the 16th century, the family supplied half of Galway's mayors, expanded their trade network, and forged strong bonds with the other merchant families that would endure for decades to come. Galway, rich and powerful, enjoyed a prolonged period of peace during the 16th century, with the Lynch family dominant.

Although it's commonly held that the Galway families stayed inside the city walls and had nothing to do with the 'wild Irish', that's not the case. In fact, it was the Gaelic families that supplied much of the produce traded by the merchant families, and when the Lynch family looked to invest their mercantile wealth, they turned to buying up land in the hinterland of Galway. By the early 1600s, the Galway Lynches, along with the Blake and Browne families, had turned much of their merchant wealth into land ownership: Between them, these three families owned more than 200,000 acres of land in Connacht, becoming the biggest landholders in the region, and their property interests became as important as their mercantile interests.

In the decades to follow, as great upheavals removed the merchant families from their dominant position in Galway, the Lynches and the other bigger merchant families invested in land as part of the great colonial expansion into the Caribbean islands. On the back of their wine trade in Europe, the Galway merchant families had started placing their sons into European cities, and with the growth of the Caribbean trade, they began to send their sons to the Caribbean to establish themselves as planters. Events in Ireland conspired to make the move to the Caribbean increasingly attractive, as Galway's ruling families found themselves on the losing side of the Confederate Wars (1641 to 1653) in Ireland. Cromwell's forces arrived to Galway in 1651 and besieged the town, and following the surrender of the town in 1652 the ruling families faced confiscation of their Irish properties.

With their properties and livelihood under threat, the wealthy Lynch merchant families of Galway left Ireland as planters and settlers, most of them bound at first for the Caribbean islands. Many of the Gaelic Irish also left Ireland for the islands as indentured servants, and it's not unlikely that there were Lynches among them. Some planters were successful and sent their sons and daughters onwards from the Caribbean to the southern states such as Virginia, as did the indentured servants. Even some slaves eventually gained their freedom and sought to become planters themselves. Often unable to get land in Barbados and elsewhere in the Caribbean, these settlers also moved west, to the English colonies.

The British settlement of the Caribbean islands began at the start of the 17th century, with settlers establishing plantations for cotton and tobacco, and importing indentured servants from Europe and slaves from Africa to do the hard work on the plantations. The merchants of Galway were not among the first planters; they simply took note of the new markets opening up in the Caribbean, for the British settlers stuck to their customary dress and diets, and the Galway merchants began sending beef, wool, butter and hides to the planters, and importing tobacco, dyes and spices and later sugar back to Europe.

From 1642 to 1649, civil war raged in England between the monarchy and the English Parliament. Oliver Cromwell's New Model Army helped to defeat the royalist forces and Cromwell was one of those who signed the death warrant of King Charles. It is recorded the Executioner of London refused to take an axe to the King. Another executioner was sought and King Charles was beheaded on 30 January 1649. According to Galway legend, the executioner was Colonel Peter Stubbers, who became one of Cromwell's officers in the Irish Confederate Wars, and was appointed Military Governor of Galway.

The last Lynch mayor of Galway, Thomas Lynch Fitz Ambrose, was deposed in 1654, and replaced by Colonel Peter Stubbers, who became the first Protestant Mayor of Galway. He also seized the Lynch townhouse at 15 High Street. (The Stubbers family occupied the house into the 20th century. The house, now known as the King's Head in commemoration of the execution of King Charles, is one of Galway's most popular pubs.) Hardiman records that Marcus Lynch FitzThomas was appointed as Sheriff under Stubbers in 1654, being the only native of Galway who changed his religion and joined the enemy: "In consequence of which, all communication was denied him by his friends during his life, and he is said to have died of a broken heart, occasioned by remorse and shame for his apostasy."

The town's property was divided and granted to Cromwell's officers, although many of the tribe families succeeded in regaining control of their properties by buying them back from the officers.

Cromwell's incursions accelerated the trend started by the Lynches, Blakes and Brownes of buying country property. Some families, deprived of their town properties, bought countryside estates from Cromwell's soldiers; even some of the families who made fortunes in Caribbean trade invested their money in land in Connaught. Many of these families would subsequently change their religion following the introduction of laws at the turn of the 18th century that deprived Catholics of ownership of land.

Cromwell's actions contributed to a strong connection between Galway and the Caribbean island of Barbados. Since the British settlement of Barbados in 1627, Irish people had voluntarily travelled to Barbados, although many more were tricked into indentured servitude by ship captains and agents promising a good life under the sun. The arrival of Cromwell in the late 1640s kicked off a new era and in 1652 resulted in a proclamation allowing the Commissioners of Ireland to transplant dangerous persons to the Commonwealth. Cromwell, who had connections to the planter families of Barbados, began seizing men, women and children and deporting them to the island as indentured servants.

In Galway, deportation to Barbados served several purposes. It emptied the town of its Catholic inhabitants, provided an income for the Military Governor and his officers, and provided labour to the plantation owners. Even as this trade in Irish servants was booming, a profound changes was taking place in the Caribbean. From the late 16th century, the main crops grown by planters were tobacco and cotton but with competition from north American plantations depressing prices in the early 17th century, Dutch planters introduced sugar cane to the islands around 1640, and planters quickly switched to sugar plantations.

Sugar quickly became such a lucrative product that it pushed out all other crops, and the labour provided by indentured servants was not enough to meet the demand for sugar, so the planters vastly increased the trade in slaves from Africa to provide the intensive labour required on the sugar plantations, and over the next century the island became the richest of the British colonies. The tribe families, being pushed out of their lucrative position in Galway society, contrived to join the sugar rush.

Galway merchants were already dealing directly with the Caribbean islands. They experience a great boom during the period from 1660 to 1720 as the main suppliers of provisions to the Caribbean islands, shipping vast quantities of beef, butter, cheese, fish and even potatoes. The profits to be made from sugar plantations were so vast that it was economical to import foodstuff from Ireland for planters and slaves alike. Yet the canny Galway merchants managed to get in on all sides of the trade. Just as they had placed family members along the Atlantic costs, they began to invest in plantation land in the Caribbean islands. The Blake and Lynch families, often working in cooperation, were able to generate great profits from the sugar trade. Nicholas Lynch, owner of plantations on Antigua and St. Christopher, married Catherine Blake, the daughter of the wealthy Montserrat plantation owner John Blake, and inherited Blake's plantation on his death in 1692. In London, the families established Blake & Lynch, one of the great sugar commission houses, establishing a family presence at each point of the sugar trade. In effect, the families were supplying products from Ireland to the Caribbean, and supplying products from the Caribbean back to Ireland, Britain and the European Continent.

The 1678 census of Montserrat records 10 Lynch families as merchants or planters, and the other Galway tribes were represented. By 1720, the thirty largest landowners in Montserrat controlled almost 80% of the land on the island, and more than half of those landowners were Irish, with the Galway tribes strongly represented. In Montserrat, the Lynches owned 360 acres of land and 121 slaves.

Irish families were so prevalent in Montserrat during the 17th century that academic Donald Akenson used the island as a case study to examine the behaviour of Irish colonists. Although it's commonly held that the Irish were a colonised people rather than colonisers, some Irish were indeed colonisers in the Caribbean, the Americas and Australia. Akenson's book *If The Irish Ran The World: Montserrat 1630-1730* concluded that the majority Irish colonists on the island were every bit as effective as colonial overlords as the English. Along with Montserrat, the tribe families were most commonly represented in Jamaica and Barbados. The early Galway planter families in Barbados included the Blakes, Frenches and Lynches, all of whom maintained their allegiance to the 'tribes' and continued to marry into other tribe families.

Thousands of formerly indentured servants who had left Ireland (and the oversight of the tribe families) gained their freedom in the Caribbean only to find that the tribe families had bought up the best land. These poor Irish, unable to buy land in the face of fierce competition for the riches provided by the sugar trade, began to move again, to other islands in the Caribbean or to the north American mainland, as early as the 1670s.

It's likely that the merchant Lynches and Gaelic Lynches were among those who moved from Barbados to Virginia and North Carolina, for the name Lynch starts to appear in colonial records from the late 17th century. Once settled in the colonies, the Lynch families established plantations and bought slaves to work the land. From North Carolina and Virginia, the Lynches moved with the frontier, and eventually moved throughout the southern states.

Other Lynch families remained in Barbados and gained a stronghold, becoming landowners and slaveholders, and in some cases, agents. In the *Barbados Mercury* of February 1766, Anthony Lynch & Sons, merchants and town agents, advertised the auction of "270 choice Whidah and Popo slaves" from their yard on High Street in Bridgetown.

Although the tribes were losing their preeminent place in Galway society, records show that upon emigration they maintained their historical practice of co-operation and marriage between families to exploit the trade triangle between the Caribbean, France and Ireland. Through this transatlantic network, news filtered back to Ireland about which places were lucrative and likely to provide an income for fresh emigrants.

NEW EMPIRES

Many of the great modern empires grew rich on the back of the brutal and brutalising process of slavery. In the Caribbean, the conquerors killed off the native Carib people, and began bringing slaves from Africa to work their tobacco plantations. With the rise of the sugar business and its massive profits, demand for slaves to do backbreaking work of cutting sugar cane increased. Various writers have argued that slavery was not perceived as wrong at the time, but the evidence contradicts this. Enslaved Africans threw themselves off ships in an effort to escape, and ran away whenever possible. Although the antislavery movement did not become formalised until the late 18th century, there had always been voices of conscience calling for an end to the practice.

In the Caribbean in particular, the brutality meted out to slaves was shocking. Several members of the Lynch clan were slaveholders in the Caribbean and the southern colonies. Government policy in England encouraged white settlers to go to the Caribbean islands. In the Jamaican Land Register of 1754, for instance, we find that William Lynch Joseph was granted 300 acres in Portland parish. The Jamaican Almanac of 1816 lists three Lynch families who owned hundreds of slaves and hundreds of acres of land. Just as not all Lynches were members or former members of the merchant aristocracy, neither were all the Lynches in Jamaica slaveholders. Some must have been ordinary people who arrived to the islands as indentured servants, and there's no doubt that there was significant intermarriage between white Irish and black Africans.

One record from Jamaica in 1787 mentions "John Lynch a free mulatto, Elizabeth his wife a free quadroon woman, Grace Anne Lynch, Elizabeth Banton Lynch, Mark Lynch, Eleanor Banton Lynch, Margaret Banton Lynch, Frances Jane Lynch, John Saunders Lynch, Benjamin Banton Lynch, Priscilla Lynch & William Lynch born in lawful wedlock to the said Elizabeth to the same rights and privileges under certain restrictions." The descriptions reflect the obsession with racial division. A mulatto had one white and one black parent, while a quadroon had three white grandparents.

Records and fok memory recall that the treatment meted out to slaves was shocking and brutal. In the Vestry records of the parish of Trelawny, we have this note from 30 September 1789: "Resolved that the Church Wardens to pay Michael Lynch the sum of Two Pounds for his trouble in burning a Negro slave, the property of Edward Jackson, Esq., pursuant of his sentence." As we'll see when we look at slavery in the United States, the emergence of 'lynching' is rooted in the notion that slaves were property, to be disposed of as their owners saw fit.

Those who would consign these matters to the past must note that the historical injustices of slavery still resonate, and representatives of descendants of slaves and entire nations continue to agitate for some kind of compensation for these injustices. In recent years, researchers have uncovered records of compensation paid out by the British Empire after the abolition of slavery, only to find that many of the wealthiest families in the United Kingdom gained much of their wealth as a result not only of slavery but from its abolition. When the British Empire abolished slavery, the government proceeded to pay out £20 million in compensation to the former slave-owning families. For instance John Gladstone, father of the 19th century prime minister William Gladstone, had owned 2,508 slaves across nine plantations. He was paid £106,769 in compensation, the equivalent of £83 million in modern money. Hundreds of other wealthy families were similarly compensated, while the former slaves received nothing for their years of free labour and brutal treatment.

Fourteen Lynch families in Jamaica, Antigua and Barbados received compensation for freeing slaves. Andrew Henry Lynch received £1,232 for 85 slaves, while most of the others owned between one and five slaves. It's a matter of historical record that many of the Irish families that emigrated to the Caribbean later moved on to the North American mainland when prices for land in the Caribbean islands went out of their reach. Those families tended to move to the southern states, from Virginia down to South Carolina and across to Texas, and many of them became slaveowners, albeit on a small scale.

In the most recent US census, 114,448 people are listed under the surname Lynch, with 12,852 identifying themselves as 'non-Hispanic Black only'. As Lynch was almost exclusively an Irish name, it's likely that many black people with the name of Lynch have the name as a result of their 19th century forebears being former slaves who took the name Lynch from their former owners.

With the end of the Civil War in 1865, the Emancipation Proclamation was declared throughout the southern states that had previously resisted the proclamation, and slaveowners were compelled to free their slaves. At that point, former slaves took surnames for themselves. Some reverted to names remembered from Africa; others adopted names of famous persons (such as Washington or Jackson); some took the name of Freeman or the name of their work (e.g. Cotton) while many took the name of their former slavemasters.

We know that Lynching and Lynch Law had entered colloquial language by the 1840s or 1850s, so it's likely that the phrase was well known among enslaved people, and it's hard to imagine that freed slaves would willingly choose the name Lynch. Yet slaves were not permitted to move around freely and communication was limited between plantations so it's also possible that many took the name without realising the terror that attached to it. In any case, they had little choice in the matter.

As the 1850 US census contains a 'slave schedule' that records the details (but not the names) of slaves under the name of the slaveholders, we have some idea of the numbers of people held by various Lynches throughout the southern states. These records indicate that 128 separate persons with the surname of Lynch owned 1147 slaves across the 14 southern states. The list below reflects the numbers of Lynches who owned slaves in 1850, with many owning a small number of slaves and others owning hundreds of people. First is the state, followed by the number of Lynches who were slaves owners, followed by the total number of slaves: In Alabama, five men owned 43 slaves; in Arkansas, two men owned four slaves; in Delaware one man owned one slave; in Georgia, 13 men owned 105 slaves; in Kentucky, 12 men owned 39 slaves; in Louisiana, five men owned 13 slaves; in Maryland, 16 men owned 86 slaves; in Mississippi, nine men owned 316 slaves; in Missouri, seven men owned 36 slaves; North Carolina, seven men owned 39 slaves; in South Carolina, 19 men owned 70 slaves; in Virginia, 31 men owned 195 slaves; in Tennessee, seven men owned 31 slaves and in Texas, three men owned 47 slaves.

Ironically, or otherwise, an analysis of the slave schedule shows that second most common name (after John) among the Lynch slaveowners was William Lynch. Between them, eleven William Lynches owned 272 slaves, and one William Lynch of Mississippi was the single biggest slaveowner with 184 slaves. Willie Lynch, as we'll see later, became a legend of late 20th century black America.

THOMAS LYNCH

With the restoration of Charles II to the English throne in 1660, the laws suppressing Catholic rights and ownership were overturned, but the Galway tribes would never regain their dominant position. In 1691, with the victory of King William, a Protestant ruling class in Ireland pushed to increase their control of the country and so began the era of Protestant Ascendancy. Penal laws denied land ownership to Catholic families, and the many tribe families who had bought land in the vicinity of Galway changed their religion from Catholic to Protestant and became part of the ascendancy class. Around the turn of the 18th century, several branches of the Lynch family set out for the New World.

One of those was Jonas or Jonack Lynch, who arrived from Galway to South Carolina in the late 17th century. A plaque erected in Rivertown, South Carolina in 2010 states that Jonack Lynch arrived in 1677, though various family histories give different dates for his arrival. (It appears that Lynch was one of the ancestors of former US president Jimmy Carter.) *The Historical and Genealogical Magazine of South Carolina* records that Jonah Lynch arrived to South Carolina on board the ship Blessing with two servants, in 1679, and had been awarded a grant of 780 acres in 1682. Lynch apparently named his plantation Blessing after the ship.

Jonas Lynch's land was adjacent to that of Sir Nathaniel Johnson, an Englishman who had served as governor of the Leeward Islands from 1686 to 1689, and then migrated to the colony of South

Carolina, where he was appointed governor. It's possible that Nathaniel's daughter Margaret married Jonas Lynch, although there are conflicting accounts. Some accounts date the marriage of Jonas and Margaret as early as 1673, before Jonah's departure for South Carolina, yet it's entirely possible that the marriage led both families to the area of the Cooper River.

Jonas Lynch had two sons, Johnson Lynch and Thomas Lynch. Johnson Lynch inherited the Blessing plantation but died in his 20s, while Thomas received a small inheritance but subsequently acquired several plantations, and experimenting with rice yields to build up a substantial empire. Thomas Lynch left his land to his son Thomas Lynch II (1727-1776), including the Hopsewee plantation that adjoined the 3,500 acre marsh island located between the northern and southern branches of the Santee river, then known as Lynch's Island. The plantation became a very profitable enterprise, and the Georgetown district was becoming one of the leading producers of rice in the US. Family records indicate that Lynch imported slaves from regions of West Africa where rice was grown, and that these Africans contributed their own knowledge of planting, harvesting and preparing the rice, helping to vastly increase yields. (If this is true, it's both remarkable and sad that he managed to coax his slaves to part with knowledge that increased his wealth while they remained enslaved.) A report from Louisiana State University states that rice production reached more than 1.5 million pounds by 1710 and more than 20 million pounds by 1720. The Georgetown region was producing half of the national crop by the mid–19th century.

As the planters imported more and more slaves to work the plantations, South Carolina became a slave society, and by the mid–1700s, more than two–thirds of the population was enslaved. In 1739, the Stono rebellion began 90 miles south of the Lynch plantation, with slaves gathering and attempting to march to freedom in Spanish Florida, 50 miles south of the Stono river. The rebellion was suppressed, with many of the slaves deported to the West Indies, but several more rebellions occurred in the following years, and the planters began carrying rifles with them.

Thomas Lynch II served in the Colonial Congress in 1765 and was appointed as an advisor to George Washington. Immensely wealthy, he sent his son Thomas Lynch III (1749-1779) to England to study at Eton College in Cambridge and then at Middle Temple in London. At the age of 21 he returned to South Carolina where he was appointed as a commander in the South Carolina regiment.

His father, Thomas Lynch II was serving in the Continental Congress of 1776, preparing the Declaration of Independence, when he was struck ill. His son, although ill, travelled to Philadelphia, where he found his father too ill to complete his work, and Thomas Lynch III signed the declaration in his father's place. The men travelled back together to South Carolina, where Thomas Lynch II died shortly afterwards. His son retired from public life, and remained ill and feverish. On the advice of his doctor, Thomas Lynch left South Carolina in 1779, bound for France by way of the West Indies. The ship was lost at sea. Before he left for France, he wrote a will stipulating that heirs of his female relatives must change their name to Lynch in order to inherit his property. He died without any heirs of his own. The plantation house at Hopsewee still stands, and was declared a national monument in 1971.

LYNCH RECONSTRUCTED

The Reconstruction Era remains a puzzling and misunderstood chapter in American history. The attempt to rebuild American society after the Civil War is largely considered to have been a failure as the southern states suffered badly from continued racism and under-investment, languishing as an agricultural backwater while the northern states powered ahead with industrialisation. Despite the emancipation of slaves at the end of the Civil War (1861-1865), Black Americans living southern states of the US endured a century of institutionalised racism up until the 1960s. The Reconstruction Era that followed the end of the Civil War was meant to give Black Americans a place in public life, and a few brave African-Americans did manage to secure themselves positions of relative power. One of those was John Roy Lynch, who served as a public representative, congressman, lawyer and historian.

Born into slavery as the son of a mother who was a slave and an Irish immigrant father, John Roy Lynch (1847-1939) didn't have the best start in life. The life of John Roy Lynch begins with a great love story. His father Patrick Lynch was born in Dublin and immigrated to the United States at a young age with his parents. With his brother Edward, Patrick Lynch left Ohio and migrated south to Louisiana where he got a job managing the Tacony cotton plantation on the Mississippi river 150 miles north of the Gulf of Mexico.

Catherine White was one of the slaves on the plantation. She was a woman of mixed race, and the daughter of parents who themselves had both African and European parents. In his autobiography *Reminiscences of an Active Life*, her son John Roy Lynch remembers her as a great beauty. Patrick Lynch and Catherine White fell in love, and had three children with the youngest boy John Roy born in September 1847. Resolving that his common-law wife and children should no longer be plantation slaves, Patrick Lynch negotiated with the plantation owner and bought Catherine White for himself. Shortly afterwards, when Alfred Vidal Davis bought the plantation, Patrick Lynch found himself out of a job and penniless, and he moved to New Orleans and lived with his brother Edward while he tried to save the money to relocate his family. Lynch fell ill in New Orleans, and returned to Tacony in 1849 to arrange his affairs. He transferred the ownership of his wife and son to a friend W.G. Deal, and died shortly afterwards.

Within months, Deal sold Catherine White and her son back into slavery, under the control of Alfred Vidal Davis. It appears from Lynch's autobiography that Davis did not treat himself and his mother harshly. "For slaveowners, they were reasonably kind, fair and considerate," wrote Lynch. John Roy served as Davis's valet until Davis was drafted into the Confederate Army in 1862. Freed at the end of the war, John Roy worked odd jobs and then found work in a photographer's studio in Natchez, across the river in Mississippi state. By 1866, he had thrown himself into learning all about the photography business and got a job running another studio, and started taking night school classes with Charles Bingham and his wife, two New Yorkers who had come south to teach freedmen, in the face of ferocious opposition from many local Whites. During lulls in business, he eavesdropped on classes at a nearby White school, and studied parliamentary law. With a rudimentary education, Lynch plunged into civic life, joining the Natchez Republican club. In 1869, recognising his abilities, the club sent him to discuss political nominations with the state's military governor Adelbert Ames.

Impressed by the young man, Ames nominated Lynch as a justice of the peace, and later that year Lynch ran for office in the Mississippi House of Representatives as a Republican. Lynch impressed colleagues with his quick mastery of parliamentary procedure and became Speaker of the House in 1873. He then joined the first wave of African-Americans serving in Congress, and argued for the Civil Rights Act of 1875. During this period, he worked as a businessman, buying and selling land in the Natchez region.

Despite the minor advances made during Reconstruction, at the end of the era in 1877 the overlords of southern society moved to frustrate any progress and introduced the Jim Crow laws and racial segregation under a 'separate but equal' mandate that forced black Americans to endure separate education and public facilities, and which would not be overturned until the famous 1954 Brown vs The Education Board Supreme Court case and subsequent cases through the 1950s and 1960s.

Lynch served in office on and off until the mid-1880s, when he was the keynote speaker at the Republican convention (and the last Black keynote speaker until 1968). He was then appointed as an auditor of the Treasury for the Navy, where served until 1893. Lynch began studying law and was called to the bar in Mississippi, but then moved to Washington D.C., where his goal was to participate in public life and to fight the discriminatory laws being imposed by southern states. With the outbreak of the Spanish-American war in 1898, he was nominated to serve as a paymaster in the US Army, and did tours of duty in Cuba and the Philippines. On his retirement he moved to Chicago as part of the great migration of southern Blacks, operated a law practice, and wrote several books.

An early revisionist, Lynch's 1913 book *The Facts of Reconstruction* was an attempt to challenge the prevailing school of the history, which told the story of reconstruction from the point of view of former slaveholders. As an insider, Lynch claimed that African-

Americans had made great contributions to American life during the Reconstruction Era. His work anticipated that the better-known African-American writer W.E.B. DuBois, whose 1935 book *Black Reconstruction in America* challenged what DuBois called the 'southern white fairytale' that blamed blacks for the failure of Reconstruction. John Roy Lynch died in Chicago in 1939, at the age of 92.

STRANGE FRUIT

The family name of Lynch came into use as a verb around the turn of the 19th century, with 'lynching' meaning to punish an accused person without trial. By the late 19th century, it had taken on a racial overtone, as lynchings were meted out mostly to black Americans by white mobs. The crime of lynching was a phenomenon particular to the United States of America, and even more particular to the southern states. To talk of 'lynching' nowadays, most people will think of it as a tool used by white Americans to brutalise black Americans in the years between Reconstruction and the Second World War. According to historian Robert Gibson, it was "a cruel combination of racism and sadism". Since those days, lynching has taken on a broader meaning largely separate from race, or even physical violence.

We find the origins of lynching in the practice of vigilantism, which existed long before the conquest of America, but took on a particular meaning as practiced by European settlers who pushed into territories in the south and west occupied by Native Americans. In newly conquered territories, there were no courts or formal criminal justice system, so local patriarchs took it on themselves to capture and punish those suspected of crimes. The most powerful people including local businessmen, the plantation owners, ranchers and merchants and their targets tended to be poor or marginalised people. Vigilantes either killed their targets or drove them out of town after a savage beating. Instances of vigilantism were recorded from the 1760s, and it's shortly after that date that 'lynch law' enters the public lexicon.

There's nothing to suggest that anything about the Lynch family inclined them to violence or racism although the concept of lynching was an expression of the vast differences in status between Americans of different race and class. 'Lynch law' can be traced to the family of Charles Lynch, who was born in Galway around 1705 and left for America at a young age seeking a new life, apparently after some argument with his family. From Galway and other ports, sea captains and their agents took willing emigrants, often penniless, and then sold them as indentured servants on arrival in the Americas as payment for the voyage. On arrival in America, Charles Lynch was bought by a man called Christopher Clark. The young servant ingratiated himself with the family and once his time was served – and it was typically seven years of indentured servitude – he married Clark's daughter and set himself up as a tobacco farmer at Chestnut Hill, where he went about buying up land and eventually amassed an estate of almost 7,000 acres. Charles Lynch had two sons. The first was also Charles Lynch, who was born around 1736 and the second was John Lynch, born around 1740. Charles Lynch Sr died around 1750, and his wife joined the Quakers, who were then coming to prominence in the area. Charles Lynch Jr inherited the family lands to the west in Bedford County, where he built a house among the meadows on the banks of the Staunton River, and called his home Green Level. The tobacco farm at Chestnut Hill went to the second son John, who would found the town of Lynchburg.

By his late 20s, the younger Charles Lynch had grown wealthy from raising tobacco and cattle farming; he owned land and African slaves and was elected to represent his area in the colonial assembly. In 1778, during the War of Independence, Lynch was commissioned as a colonel of the militia, but wasn't called into action until 1780 when the war spread into Virginia. Lynch was tipped off that the

Bedford Tories – loyal to the British crown – were conspiring to seize stores that Lynch had gathered, in advance of the arrival of the British colonial governor Charles Cornwallis. Lynch had the conspirators arrested, among them two other former Justices of the county court. With Lynch presiding, the ringleaders were sentenced to terms of imprisonment ranging from one to five years, along with fines.

Yet Lynch had exceeded his authority, as punishment for the crime of treason was only within the remit of the General Court. After the war, the Tories threatened to bring lawsuits against Lynch, who brought the matter before the Virginia legislature. The legislature retroactively indemnified Lynch against any charges, ruling that "the measures taken for that purpose may not be strictly warranted by law although justifiable from the imminence of the danger". In a letter from Charles Lynch to William Hay written in 1782 that is preserved at the Library of Virginia, the author mentions 'Lynch's law': "I am convinc'd a party there is, who by Lying, has deceived some good men to Listen to them–They are mostly Torys & such as Sanders had given Lynch's law for Dealing with the negros &c". Lynch was already conscious that his actions had generated their own extrajudicial laws, and his letter to May certainly links the actions to race.

This idea that illegal actions could in fact be justifiable slowly spread from Bedford to the rest of Virginia and became known as Lynch's Law. Over the following decades, Viriginians and other would argue back and forth about the correctness of the 'Lynch law', with many trying to frame the argument solely in judicial terms. The notion that slaveholders had ability to take the law into their own hands and to execute their slaves if necessary, was an expression of the ideology that slaves were property to be disposed of at the whim of their owners, without resort to any law.

By 1792, many suits were recorded under 'Lynch's Law' on the south side of the James river in Virginia, and the term began to spread to other states as the frontier moved west. By the 1820s and 1830s, punishments ranging from lashing and tarring and feathering to executions were being recorded across frontier towns, with references made to 'Doctor Lynch', 'Chief Justice Lynch' and 'Judge Lynch', making it clear that 'Judge Lynch' had become shorthand for summary justice. In the 1830s, the term starts to change from 'Lynch-law' to being 'lynched', which still referred to extra-judicial punishment, and could range from physical punishment to execution. Newspapers began to record the existence of vigilante groups called 'Lynch Clubs'.

In many ways, the rise of cheap newsprint and newspapers helped to popularise the terms, and newspapers tended to copy stories heard from other jurisdictions. Christopher Waldrep, author of *The Many Faces of Judge Lynch: Extralegal Violence and Punishment in America* noted that the term 'lynching' entered print culture in the early 1820s at precisely the time when Andrew Jackson ascended to the office of President. Jackson was known for killing those he considered 'enemies of the public': Waldrep believed that white Americans admired Jackson for his willingness to act decisively outside the constraints of the law.

The perception among historians of lynching has changed significantly over the years, and has been an ideological battleground in its own right. Historians in the 19th and early 20th century tended to believe that lynching was a nonracial phenomenon, while many modern historians of lynching observe that the racial dimension which we now associate with the phenomenon accelerated after the Civil War and the abolition of slavery. The recorded incidents, and the response to such incidents, shows that following the Reconstruction era, lynching was driven not by extrajudicial justice but by the drive to maintain white supremacy; black towns grew across the south, and white business owners fearing the loss of their markets used lynching to remove competitors. Black victims of lynchings were most commonly political activists or labour organisers who could be punished for their political work. Yet, almost any pretext was good enough for mob justice: charges could include verbal assault or failing to step out of the way of a white man's carriage or automobile. A favoured charge was association of black men with white women, and lynching became a means for white men to reinforce their masculine domination.

In early 20th century America, at the peak of the lynching of black Americans, a number of authors argued that the original intentions of Col. Lynch and his 18th century vigilantes were much different than those of the 20th century mobs, though some proponents of a nonracial, 'constitutional lynching' – who insisted that lynching mostly took place in thinly populated frontiers away from the courts – held heinous racial views themselves. Some authors tried to muddy the waters by claiming that 'Lynch law' came from a different and earlier era.

Writing in the 1904 edition of *American Philology*, the author Albert Matthews considered the evidence that the name 'Lynch law' variously derived from 'Mayor Lynch of Galway', the governor of Jamaica Stephen Lynch, William Lynch and Colonel Lynch. Matthews flags up the possibility that 'Lynch law' originated from one William Lynch, who claimed in 1811 that it was he who had originated and named 'Lynch law'. Matthews concludes that Colonel Charles Lynch was only one of many who committed "illegal acts" against the Tories during the War of Independence, and cannot find mention of the term 'Lynch law' prior to 1819: "Whenever we find a term containing a proper name, there seems to be an ineradicable tendency to explain the term by referring it to some person or thing of the same name. *Uncle Sam*, *Brother Jonathon*, and other examples of this process will readily occur to the reader.... In the opinion of the present writer, so far as Charles Lynch is concerned, the Scotch verdict of 'not guilty' must be rendered; and the origin of the term lynch law is yet to be determined."

The introduction of William Lynch appears to come from an article written by Edgar Allen Poe, who served a two-year tenure as assistant editor of the *Southern Literary Messenger,* based in Richmond, Virginia. Poe contributed poems, short stories and book reviews and in the issue of May 6 1838, he wrote a short piece about the interest in the origins of "Lynch's law". The law, wrote Poe, "originated in 1780, in Pittsylvania, Virginia," and its author was one "Colonel William Lynch". Poe wrote that he had been informed of this fact by a resident of Pittsylvania, "who was a member of a body formed for the purpose of carrying it into effect".

Poe followed his pronouncement with a long description, purporting to be the actual 'Lynch Law' itself, written in a faux legalistic manner. (The law is written in two sentences. One reads: "Whereas, many of the inhabitants of the county of Pittsylvania, as well as elsewhere, have sustained great and intolerable losses by a set of lawless men who have banded themselves together to deprive honest men of their just rights and property, by stealing their horses, counterfeiting, and passing paper currency, and committing many other species of villainy, too tedious to mention, and that those vile miscreants do still persist in their diabolical practices, and have hitherto escaped the civil power with impunity, it being almost useless and unnecessary to have recourse to our laws to suppress and punish those freebooters, they having it in their power to extricate themselves when brought to justice by suborning witnesses who do swear them clear — we, the subscribers, being determined to put a stop to the iniquitous practices of those unlawful and abandoned wretches, do enter into the following association, to wit: that next to our consciences, soul and body, we hold our rights and property, sacred and inviolable." Poe had in fact created this law himself, for 'Lynch's law' as such was not a law at all. Yet Poe's account subsequently influenced other historians and served to embed the truth of William Lynch's claim. Oddly enough, through this creative writing, William Lynch would eventually gain the fame he strove for, with the 'William Lynch letter'.

In 1901, three black men were lynched in Pierce City, Missouri, allegedly for the murder of a young woman in the town. After reading about the killings, Missouri-born writer Mark Twain was moved to write an essay that he titled 'The United States of Lyncherdom', decrying the phenomenon. Twain found it impossible to believe that crowds should enjoy the spectacle of lynchings. He knew of only two sheriffs in the entire south who had prevented a lynching, and despaired that he would one day see a crowd of 50,000 attend a lynching in New York, without a lawman in sight. According to the University of Virginia, Twain thought at first to publish the essay as an introduction to a book subscription history of lynching in America, but soon thought better of it. It was eventually published 13 years after his death in 1910 by Albert Bigelow Paine in *Europe and Elsewhere*.

During the period from about 1890 to 1930, the lynching of black people reached its apex, and lynching became definitively associated with anti-black violence. Lynchings relied on spectacle; they were advertised in newspapers and drew large crowds. The lynching of a single black man on a city street reverberated far and wide; it was a form of terrorism. Richard Wright, author of *Black Boy*, heard stories of lynchings as a child, which terrified him. He recalled: "The things that influenced my conduct as a Negro did not have to happen to me directly; I needed but to hear of them to feel their full effects in the deepest layers of my consciousness. Indeed, the white brutality that I had not seen was a more effective control of my behaviour than that which I knew."

The element of spectacle was bound up with the modernisation of turn-of-the-century America. Amy Louise Wood has observed that most studies of lynching in the first half of the 20th century cast the crime as an archaic relic from the Southern backwoods. Yet she points out that the high point in lynching of black people between 1890 and 1910 coincided with modernisation; the increased flow of people into cities, and the new social order put black and white people in close proximity in urban centres. Wood observed that urban life brought white and black people together in public spaces such as sidewalks, shops and public transport together; white authorities responded by performing lynchings in public spaces and effectively reclaimed these spaces as white property. These lynchings on city streets were filmed and photographed, and are predominantly urban images: bodies hang from lampposts or telegraph poles.

The taking and sharing of lynching photographs became commonplace, and people sent picture postcards of lynchings that they had witnessed. The practice became so common that in 1908 the US Postmaster General banned the cards from the mail. The antiquary James Allen collected more than 100 photographs from this era and published them in an anthology *Without Sanctuary: Lynching Photographs in America*. The historian Leon F. Litwack wrote with horror about the self-satisfied expression on the faces of some of those in the mob, even as they posed beneath black people hanging dead from a rope.

On August 6, 1930, two young black men, Thomas Shipp and Abram Smith, were arrested and charged with murder of white factory worker Claude Deeter and the rape of Mary Ball. A mob of thousands broke them out of jail and hanged the men from a tree in the town centre. Lawrence Beitler took a photograph of the dead men, surrounded by the town's citizens including children, and the photograph was printed in national and international newspapers. Abel Meeropol, a Jewish teacher in New York was so disturbed by the picture and that he wrote a poem called 'Strange Fruit':

Southern trees bear a strange fruit,
Blood on the leaves and blood on the root,
Black bodies swinging on the Southern breeze,
Strange fruit hanging from the poplar trees

Meeropol composed music for the poem, and passed it to a New York club owner, who passed it in turn to singer Billie Holliday. (The song earner Meeropol an appearance before a New York committee investigating communism in schools, who wanted to know if the communist party had paid Meeropol to write the song.) Billie Holliday made the song famous.

The meaning of 'lynching' continued to shift. While formerly thought of as a mob murder, it began to take on resonance even in the case of murders committed by one or two people. In August 1955, a 14-year-old black boy called Emmett Till was murdered by two men for allegedly flirting with a white woman. His killers were found not guilty in by an all-white jury, though they subsequently admitted their guilt to a reporter, causing outrage and leading black campaigners to push for further civil rights, believing that the legal system was fatally flawed. Two months after the September trial, Rosa Parks sparked a new civil rights movement when she refused to give up her seat on a segregated bus in Mobile, Alabama: "I thought of Emmett Till and I just couldn't go back."

In 2013, the killing of a young black man called Trayvon Martin by George Zimmerman caused a massive outcry, particularly when Zimmerman was acquitted. The NAACP (National Association for the Advancement of Colored People) called the killing a "modern-day lynching".

Although racial violence persists, lynchings committed by mobs grew far less common after the 1950s, and the expression was increasingly used in a metaphorical context. In a famous incident in 1991, black American Clarence Thomas was nominated to the

Supreme Court, and during the process he was accused of sexual harassment by attorney Anita Hill. Thomas described the resulting drama as a "high-tech lynching for uppity blacks". It was a message, Thomas said, that those who refused to bend to the old order – in this case, the notion that black Americans should profess liberal ideas – "will be lynched, destroyed, caricatured by a committee of the U.S. Senate rather than hung from a tree".

For over a century, 'lynching' was a particularly American expression of vigilantism, though it's become widely used around the world and in any given month, one can find news stories about lynchings from around the globe. In July 2014 in France, the word lynching featured in stories where a mob nearly killed a Roma teenager suspected of burglary; when Indian mill workers killed a boss who refused to increase their pay; and elsewhere in India, when villagers killed a man accused of stealing cars. The term is also widely used in a political contexts, often in the context of a wholesale change of opinion about a political candidate or official. For example, in 2013 New Jersey Governor Chris Christie was hailed as a hero for his actions during Hurricane Sandy, and a potential nominee for President, only to be disgraced several months later over alleged misuse of hurricane relief funds. His supporters described the charges against him as a 'political lynching'. When a Florida judge ruled in July 2014 that he would overturn a ban on same-sex marriages, one outraged activist described the judge's decision as a "judicial lynching of the people of Florida". The name of the punishment first named by Charles Lynch has not only endured but has grown in scope, meaning and geographical reach.

THE TEXANS

From the 1840s onwards, we can trace the arrival of many Lynches to Texas, mostly from Virginia and other southern states. The independent Republic of Texas established in 1836 offered opportunities and many of the Lynches who moved south came with funds to establish themselves as farmers or ranchers. A contested territory since the arrival of the Spanish conquistadors, Texas hosted many Native American tribes, but the state eventually fell to Mexico when the country won its independence from Spain in 1821. The Mexican authorities opened up Texas to settlers, and more than 30,000 Anglos streamed in from the US and Germany, drawn by opportunities for ranching and cotton farming. Conflict grew between the authorities and settlers, and turned into a military confrontation in 1835 when the Mexican troops tried to seize a cannon in Gonzales. One of the newly arrived settlers to join the Texas forces was Joseph Penn Lynch, the grandson of the infamous William Lynch.

The name of William Lynch of Pittsylvania appears more than once in this book, for he was reported by Edgar Allen Poe to be the father of 'Lynch-law'. William Lynch's descendants won and lost fortunes in war and business, and the history of this one family in some way carries on the family tradition of mercenary business, although their own family history might suggest that they were patriots rather than mercenaries.

William Lynch of Pittsylvania, Virginia was born sometime in the 1740s, and received a number of land grants in Pittsylvania in 1774 and 1779; he also purchased land in the county and represented Pittsylvania County in the Virginia Legislature in 1787. Interviewed in 1811 by the diarist Andrew Ellicot, William Lynch claimed to have invented the term 'Lynch-law'. Lynch told Ellicot stories about torturing prisoners and his cruelty appalled Ellicot, who never published his diaries. However the story was taken up several years later by Edgar Allen Poe, in what's now widely regarded as one of Poe's many hoaxes, so William Lynch did manage to insert his name into the historical record and his name frequently appears in discussions of the origins of Lynch law and lynching. The history of William Lynch's descendants is not so well known, but they rose to great heights in Texas society.

William Lynch's son William grew up in Simpson, Kentucky, where sometime around 1810 he had a child called Joseph Penn Lynch. The boy moved to Texas some time in the late 1820s or early 1830s and settled close to Waco, Texas, and took work initially as a schoolteacher, but left his job to join the growing rebellion against Mexican rule. He began serving with Philip Coe's Company of Rangers in 1835, and in the autumn of 1835 he became a member of Company E in the First Regiment of the Texas Volunteers, and fought in the Battle of San Jacinto after initially fighting in the siege of Bexar (San Antonio). He was honourably discharged from the army at the end of May 1836 and for his efforts, Joseph Penn Lynch was rewarded with large tracts of land in several counties in Limestone, Texas, 100 miles north of the state capital Austin.

For his part in the storming and capture of Bexar from December 5 to 10, 1836, he was granted 640 acres of land close to Houston, and for his stints of military service between October 1 1835 and September 13 1836, he received a further grant of 960 acres, in three packets of 320 acres, for a total of 1600 acres. One land grant was 20 miles west of Waco and another was 20 miles to the east, while the third parcel was 100 miles to the south, in Austin County. He briefly returned to teaching and married one of his pupils, Mary Miller, who was ten years his junior. As his biographer notes, as a 'true son of Kentucky', he had a great love of horses and he raised horses, cattle and sheep on his three ranches.

He had seven children and his two eldest boys William and Andrew both fought in the Civil War with the Texas Rangers. His fourth child Laura married Neal Davidson and moved to live with him in his native Louisiana. When Neal Davidson died at 34 years of age, Laura took her family back to their pioneer roots in Groesbeck, Texas, in the centre of the state. The young Lynch Davidson herded sheep after school and when he graduated at the age of 15, he started work at a local timber mill. After working as a roustabout, the boy moved into selling timber and at the age of 23, he opened his own timber yard in Laredo, Texas, on the Rio Grande river. This venture grew into the Continental Timber Company, which in turn grew into an enterprise made up of retail yards all across Texas. Lynch Davidson's timing was good, for lumber along with cotton dominated the state's industry from the 1880s into the late 1920s, when it was surpassed by the oil boom. By 1921, Lynch Davidson had moved to Houston where he combined his various enterprises into Lynch Davidson & Company, serving as president.

He first ran for political office in 1918, serving as State Senator and then briefly as Lieutenant Governor of the state in 1920, and his political career was marked by an interest in the state railroads, a traditional interest of the powerful timber and oil barons of Texas: Davidson was known as the Lumber King of the South. By the time he died in 1952, his obituary writers could look back on a career distinguished by connections at the highest level of business and politics, remarking on his membership of the Houston Club, the Thalian Club, the Houston Country Club and the River Oaks Country Club, where he mingled with his fellow Houstonians, many of whom he knew from his directorships at the Lumberman's National Bank of Houston, the Second National Bank and the Great Southern Life Insurance Company.

ELIZA LYNCH: QUEEN OF PARAGUAY

Until recently she was virtually unknown in Ireland, the land of her birth, but Eliza Lynch is one of the most infamous names in Paraguay and South America. Widely and unfairly blamed for causing the War of the Triple Alliance, her infamy extended into modern times. A 1975 book by Alan Brodsky was titled *Madam Lynch and Friend: the true account of an Irish adventuress and the dictator of Paraguay who destroyed that American Nation* in which Brodsky claimed that Lynch had been a prostitute in a Paris brothel before rising to fame. In the 1988 book *The World's Wickedest Women*, author Margaret Nichols called Eliza Lynch a whore, thief, torturer and killer. An interested reader looking back through histories of Paraguay would find similar aspersions being cast over her character.

It's only in the last few years that she has been enjoying a gradual rehabilitation in the popular imagination, in part because the magnitude of her alleged crimes seems so out of proportion. As the confidante, lover and mother to at least six children of the Paraguayan dictator Francisco Solano López, her name is forever attached to the War of The Triple Alliance, the most destructive war in South American history.

Francisco Solano López followed his grandfather and father as leader of Paraguay, serving as commander-in-chief of the army under his father. Francisco was dispatched to Europe in 1853 to procure weapons and other military supplies, along with means to modernise Paraguay. It was in Paris that he met Eliza Lynch. Eliza

Lynch was born in Co. Cork in 1833, daughter of a Dr. John Lynch and his wife Jane Elizabeth Lloyd. Shortly before or during the start of the great Irish famine of the 1840s, she left Ireland with her family and moved to France, where she went to school and learned to speak French, play the piano, and carry herself as a stylish young woman. At 16, she was married to Xavier Quatrefages, a French office who appeared to have tricked her into the relationship, and subsequently declined to be seen with her in public. She escaped from the relationship after Quatrefages had been posted to Algeria, and returned to Paris, where she met the fabulously wealthy Francisco Solano López and began a relationship. At 21 years of age she was, in the words of her biographer Michael Lillis, "the unofficial Queen of Paris".

She left Paris for Paraguay, where she served for the next 15 years as the unofficial first lady of Paraguay, bearing the children of López. Due to jealousy within López's immediate family at his likely ascent to power, his brothers had turned the elite of Paraguayan society against Eliza Lynch, although the particular and peculiar history of Paraguay meant that unmarried mothers were common and the ordinary people of Paraguay were not scandalised by López's relationship. While López awaited his turn as leader, Eliza Lynch led a life mostly out of view of the public, while entertaining foreign leaders and dignitaries, and building her own life as a businesswoman with investments in tobacco and cattle. As her biographers note, her name does not appear at all in the government records of the López era. She was simply written out of official history. However, as she introduced European customs, music (such as the polka) and fashion, she was apparently something of a figure of fascination to Paraguayan women, in yet another case where the official history bears little resemblance to popular history.

In 1862, following the death of his father, Francisco Solano López became the ruler of Paraguay. He had inherited a fabulously wealthy country from his father, but he would leave behind an impoverished and destroyed nation within a decade. The leader of the landlocked nation desired direct access to the sea, and sought to seize part of neighbouring Brazil. López had built up a standing army bigger than the combined armies of Brazil, Argentina and Uruguay, and in 1864 he launched the war that would be known as the War of The Triple Alliance. There is ample evidence that López, deeply influenced by Napoleon and his empire-building, planned the war for many years. He militarised the country, and provoked the war.

Yet López's military planning proved inadequate, and following some initial victories, the allies of Brazil, Argentina and Uruguay gained the upper hand. By 1872, the Paraguayan army had been worn down to a few thousand men, and in the grim surroundings of Cerro Cerá, López and his retinue, including Eliza Lynch, were finally vanquished by Brazilian troops. López was killed, and Lynch claimed protection as an English citizen. Spared from death, she buried López and their eldest son with her bare hands. (The scene is engraved on her gravestone in Asunción.) The governments of Argentina, Uruguay and Brazil allowed her safe passage through their territories. She departed South America from Rio de Janeiro, bound for Falmouth on the ship City of Limerick. Modern estimates suggest that Paraguay lost 90% of its male population of 500,000 over the six years of the Paraguayan wars, and 50% of its women and children, making it the most destructive in the modern era, and a complete disaster for the country.

Yet, before that war had ended, many of the influential chroniclers of the time sought to portray Eliza Lynch as the cause of the war, a European outsider who had corrupted the Paraguayan leader with her greed and ambition, though there is scant evidence that she had any political influence over her lover. In 1869, a former English army apothecary called George Frederick Masterson issued

Seven Eventful Years in Paraguay, proclaiming of Eliza Lynch: "That lady occupied a very prominent place eventually in Paraguayan affairs and, I believe, by her evil counsels was the remote cause of the terrible war which has utterly depopulated the country."

In 1870, the 350-page book *Elisa Lynch* by journalist Hector Varela became a bestseller in Paraguay: Varela charged that "She changes lovers as often as she changes her clothes." It was part of a general charge that Eliza Lynch was once a prostitute. In *A History of Paraguay*, Charles A. Washburn, the American ambassador to Paraguay writes: "She belonged to that class of woman so numerous in Paris, always on the watch for strangers with long purses and vicious habits… To the bad, selfish, pitiless woman may be ascribed many of the numberless acts of cruelty of her paramour."

In the 1874 book *Dictadura de Mariscal López*, author Vicente Villa Vicencio continued the assault on Lynch's reputation, and his work served as the basis for Héctor Francisco Decoud's *Elisa Lynch de Quatrefages*. In this account, she was purchased by López from Quatrefages, and the book quotes Manuel Balboa: "How could that woman take her place among the immortals who was no more than the whore who incorporated all the degrading vices of European corruption."

Much of the acrimony surrounding Eliza Lynch was due to her extensive purchase of lands and properties before and during the war, and by modern standards she was at one stage a billionaire and one of the biggest female landowners in the world. Yet there were two parts to this particular story. She bought 37,500 acres of land in the Chaco wilderness and north of the Apa river, large tracts of land in areas of Paraguay contested by Brazil and Argentina but the intention of Lynch's large-scale land purchases appears to be to obstruct the seizure of Paraguayan land by bringing it into private ownership. On the other hand, she had also planned a future past the war and had started to accumulate properties with her own money, amassing 23 houses and building sites in Asunción intended as the basis for a major development. Although she lost almost everything in the flight from Paraguay, Lynch believed that her assets had been unfairly seized, and took legal actions to recover them.

Back in the UK, she began proceedings in the Edinburgh courts to recover money that she had entrusted to Dr. William Stewart, the Scottish-born Paraguayan Surgeon-General and personal doctor to López. Lynch estimated the money due to her by Stewart at £40,000, but eventually she settled for £7,000. In 1875 she returned to visit Asunción, lured by the prospect of recovering some of her properties, only to find out that President Gill had hoped to gain information on the whereabouts of Paraguay's missing national treasure, which he believed to be secretly buried somewhere. Unable to convince the President that she did not know where the treasure was, she was banished from the country. She then began writing *Exposition: A Protest by Eliza Lynch*, documenting her years with López and denying the supposedly corrosive influence that she exercised over him. She wrote: "For a long time I maintained a profound silence, though my name had for six years been attacked by determined enemies, by individuals who sought riches by writing pamphlets and books of appalling filth, representing me as the very essence of prostitution and scandal, as though I were one of those human beasts who seek satisfaction in the extermination of society itself." She died in Paris in July 1886.

In 1961, with her reputation in Paraguay restored under the dictator General Alfredo Stroessner, her remains were exhumed from Père Lachaise cemetery in Paris and taken to Paraguay. Stroessner's plan to re-bury her alongside López was vetoed by the Catholic Church, and she was finally laid to rest in the Military Museum.

The wider rehabilitation of Eliza Lynch owes much to *The Lives Of Eliza Lynch: Scandal and Courage*, by former Irish diplomat Michael Lillis and historian Ronan Fanning, who observe that much of badness ascribed to Lynch was invented by her enemies. In recent years, the rehabilitated Eliza Lynch has become the subject of plays, documentaries and films.

LYNCH OF MERRILL LYNCH

As we've seen with Germyn Lynch, there are some businesses where investors like to see constant innovation, but there are other businesses where investors prefer to see conservative and prudent management. Banking belongs in the second category. For 90 years, the American investment company Merrill Lynch had grown steadily into one of the country's biggest and most respected institutions. Following the technology bubble of 2000 and the events of 9/11, Wall Street looked for new ways to make money. Merrill Lynch didn't want to fall behind. Using powerful computers, brilliant mathematicians had invented apparently fool-proof methods for managing high-risk investments, and banks were loading up on these new high-yielding bonds which blended high-risk mortgages with other safer investments and still managed to secure ratings of low–risk products.

Merrill Lynch has its fingers in many international pies. It served as an underwriter for Anglo Irish Bank bonds and as a corporate broker for Allied Irish Banks, at the time the two biggest banks in Ireland. In a briefing note in March 2008, the Merrill Lynch analyst Phil Ingram suggested that a banking crisis was looming. Merrill Lynch's Irish clients complained, and Merrill Lynch quietly gutted the report.

Yet the report was accurate, for things were indeed looking very ropey inside the Irish banking world. Six months after Ingram's report, the Irish government brought in Merrill Lynch as an adviser.

For €7 million, the bank wrote a seven-page report explaining that the Irish banks were well funded, and would cost €16 billion to fully recapitalise in the event of a shock. That month, the Irish government introduced a blanket banking guarantee scheme. Merrill's report turned out to be nonsense. The cost of the banking guarantee turned out to be €64 billion, four times their estimate. So began a cycle of disasters for all parties.

Merrill Lynch was massively overexposed to subprime mortgages, and by late 2008 it was facing catastrophic losses, and was forced to enter takeover talks with Bank of America; early in 2009, Merrill Lynch was folded into the bank's wealth management division. By the end of 2010, the Irish government was forced to seek help from the EU and the IMF, and was forced in return to introduce a radical programme of financial cutbacks and social reforms.

It's reasonable to suppose that bond salesman Edmund C. Lynch never imagined the day when his bank would one day be chief financial advisor to the country of his ancestors. The early incarnation of Merrill Lynch, after all, was built on the prudent selling of financial services to the man in the street, and Edmund was its pessimist-in-chief and bellwether of overreach. Born in Baltimore in 1885 to Richard Hinkle Lynch and Jennie Vernon Smith, Edmund Lynch was given a first name long popular among the Lynches of Galway. From a prosperous family, he attended Johns Hopkins University in 1907 and joined the Phi Gamma Delta fraternity. He graduated at the age of 22 and moved to New York where he found a job as a salesman at the Liquid Carbonic Company, which manufactured soda fountains, the dispensers of carbonated soft drinks that survive relatively unchanged a century later and are staples of fast-food restaurants and convenience stores. In 1909, Lynch met Charles Merrill, an ambitious young Floridian who had moved to New York to work for commercial paper house George H. Burr & Co.

Charles Merrill was born in Florida in 1885, and briefly attended college in Amherst, Massachusetts, before moving to upstate New York to work for a textile firm owned by George Burr. On learning of Merrill's financial abilities, Burr brought Merrill to Wall Street to create a bond department for Burr's investment bank. Merrill hired Lynch to come and work for him at the bank. In 1912, Burr underwrote the initial public offering for shares in the Kresge chain store. In the process of creating a bond market for George H. Burr & Co., Charles Merrill discerned that there were thousands of potential small investors who were being overlooked by the bigger Wall Street banks, and Merrill decided to make those investors his customers.

In 1914, Charles Merrill struck out on his own, and rented an office on Wall Street. He persuaded Edmund Lynch to join him and named the firm Merrill, Lynch & Co., and the new business concentrated on the emerging chain store business, and on selling to a broad market of small investors. The timing was good: Following the First World War, US citizens embarked on a decade-long embrace of the stock market and consumer culture, driven by new mass production techniques, mass advertising campaigns driven by the emerging mass media of radio, and instalment buying that allowed people to purchase items previously out of their reach. According to company lore, Edmund Calvert Lynch was the company pessimist, alive to dangers and overreach, while Merrill played the optimist.

It was the era of the first chain-stores: Charles Merrill co-founded a chain called Safeway, which is now one of the three biggest chain stores in America, and Merrill Lynch financed the development of several other chain stores, selling securities for J.C. Penney and S.S. Kresge (which became K-Mart). Merrill grew alarmed by the speculative boom in the late 1920s, and advised his clients to sell off their securities. Again, according to company lore, his opinion was so out of tune with the times that Merrill sought psychiatric advice. The psychiatrist was convinced, and asked Merrill to sell his shares. Edmund Lynch disagreed with his partner's analysis, but deferred to Merrill's judgement, and the company survived the crash.

With small investors wiped out, Merrill Lynch concentrated on investment banking during the 1930s. Edmund Lynch died in 1938 while in London on business. Charles Merrill was able to resurrect the brokerage business and the firm prospered again after the Second World War, offering its rationale as 'bringing Wall Street to Main Street'. The firm established a vast brokerage network and added millions of investors as clients, giving it a direct outlet for its securities. It grew into one of the biggest banks in the world by the time of its eventual collapse in 2009. Winthrop Smith, the son of one of Merrill and Lynch's first partners and himself a company manager, lambasted company boss Stan O'Neal for losing sight of the company's mission, and basic investing advice such as being able to understand the product being invested in. Famously, the high-risk investments known as Collateralised Debt Obligations (CDOs) being snapped up by the banks following the tech stocks crash were so complicated that their issuers were hiring physics and mathematics graduates to write the complex algorithms behind the products, as even expensively educated banking graduates couldn't understand them. Incidentally, one of the best-known investors in America is Peter Lynch, a manager of the Fidelity funds. Lynch often offered pithy quotes that may have been useful to Merrill Lynch and other investment giants, such as never investing in an idea that you can't explain with a crayon.

It was a period that the company and O'Neal would like to forget. While we labour under the illusion that everything 'ends up' on the internet, there are in fact filters at work. Revisiting his work about Merrill Lynch, the financial journalist Robert Peston noticed in July 2014 that his 2007 article about Stan O'Neal and Merrill Lynch had been removed from Google's archives as a result of a 'right to be forgotten' ruling by the European Court of Justice. Now it's the case that the facts become legend.

CHE AND GRAY AT THE BAG OF PIGS

In December 2014, the US and Cuba began normalising relations, after 54 years of frozen ties between the neighbours. Much of that bad blood can be traced back to a single incident, but the failed invasion of Cuba in 1961 commonly known as the 'Bay of Pigs' has never really been given the historical attention it deserves, possibly because it was such a convoluted and messy affair. Lined up against Fidel Castro's young administration was an unlikely alliance of Cuban criminals, US mob leaders and their hit men, renegade CIA officers, and the nervy young leaders and officials of the Kennedy administration. Cuba of the 1950s was a kind of gangster's paradise. Under Cuban leader Fulgencio Batista, Cuba became a playground for the world's wealthy, where the Mafia ran casinos, brothels and drugs. Havana was the main transshipment point for the Mafia's transatlantic heroin trade into the USA: opium from Turkey came through Lebanon into the mob laboratories in Sicily and Marseilles where it was turned into heroin and smuggled into the USA through Cuba. US businesses controlled the island's sugar and mineral industries.

All of this changed in 1959 when Fidel Castro's forces overthrew Batista's regime. The mafia lost their casinos and their lucrative smuggling base, and US businesses saw their Cuban organisations nationalised. Although at first it wasn't clear what way Castro would swing, he soon aligned himself with the Soviet Union, to the alarm of the United States government. The CIA, US corporations and the

Mafia pushed for a quick invasion, only to be slowed by the 1960 US election. Once in power, the Kennedy government vacillated, wary of a plan that had been cooked up under Eisenhower's administration. When the plan was finally approved in early April of 1961, the stage was set for an encounter with the Cubans on one side, and the Mafia, the CIA and anti-Castro Cubans on the other side. In one of history's stranger coincidences, the military leaders of both sides were Lynches. One was a devoted anti-communist, and the other a devoted anti-capitalist and enemy of imperialism.

On the US side was the CIA paramilitary commander Grayston L Lynch, who led the seaborne invasion force of Cuban exiles into the Bay of Pigs. On the other side was Che Guevara, son of Ernesto Guevara Lynch, who raced with his troops to take on the invaders. It was a farcical and tragic encounter. The Bay of Pigs turned out to be a terrible landing spot. The landing force was held up first by coral reefs, before encountering stiff resistance from a local militia, and it was then picked off by the Cuban air force. Fooled by a CIA decoy, Che Guevara's forces arrived at a spot 350 kilometres to the west of the Bay of Pigs and completely missed the three-day battle. Most of the Cuban invaders were killed or captured but Grayston Lynch escaped and returned to the USA, while Guevara showed up after the battle to claim victory. The legacy of the failed invasion set off a chain of events that included the Cuban Missile crisis, the assassination of President John F. Kennedy in Dallas, and the 1968 killing of Che Guevara in a Bolivian jungle.

So who were these two remarkable Lynches, and what fate drove them to become such implacable enemies? Grayston Lynch was born in Texas in 1923, the son of a farmer and oil driller whose family and military heritage we can trace back to 18th century Ireland. Grayston Lynch's ancestor George Lynch was born in Ireland, possibly in Ulster, in 1748, and married a Scottish woman called Margaret McCorkle before emigrating to York, Pennsylvania in 1770. Their grandson Enoch grew up in Virginia and moved south to Texas with several of his siblings. A Baptist preacher, Enoch settled in Hunt County in north-central Texas where his son James and grandson Henry Thomas were born. When the oil boom came to Texas, Henry T. Lynch supplemented his work as a ranch hand with some freelance work as an oil driller. Henry's third child Grayston was born in Gilmer, Texas in June 1923.

By his teenage years, Grayston Lynch was already tall and strong, and he enlisted in the US Army in 1938 at the age of fifteen. He fought in the second world war, serving as a platoon sergeant, and landed on Omaha Beach on D-Day. Badly injured in the fighting, he spent five years recovering in hospital. After his release from hospital he earned a degree in political science at the University of Maryland in 1953, and then served in the Korean War before rising to the role of captain with the 77th Special Forces Group in Laos. (In the movie *The A-Team*, several of the CIA agents use the name Lynch and in the television series, the character of Colonel Lynch was reputedly based on Grayston Lynch.) According to his autobiography, Lynch was on the point of retirement from the army in 1960 when a connection in the CIA persuaded him to join the agency as a case officer. Lynch agreed. The emergence of Fidel Castro as Cuban leader following the overthrow of Batista in 1959 was causing alarm in Washington, and the CIA had been tasked with an invasion of the country once the 1960 election between Kennedy and Nixon was out of the way. Lynch was put in charge of the invasion, an enormous task for a new officer, which suggests that Lynch had already been involved with the CIA before his official recruitment. As the CIA waited for Eisenhower's Vice-President Richard Nixon to take his rightful place in the White House, Grayston Lynch and his team co-leader William 'Rip' Robertson began assembling a force of Cuban exiles who had been pouring out of Cuba into Miami, raging at the changes sweeping across the island under Fidel Castro and Castro's second-in-command Ernesto Guevara. Grayston Lynch studied the make up of the Cuban Army, but it's unlikely that he realised that its commander Che Guevara was also a Lynch.

In fact, Che Guevara himself took no particular pride in his Irish origins, although his precise genealogy was a source of agitation to his supporters and detractors. Was Che Guevara one of the Gaelic Lynches with a revolutionary anti-imperialist tradition? Or did he belong to the solid merchant class of Anglo-Irish origin? The Irish forebears of Ernesto 'Che' Guevara were the Lynches of Lydican Castle, on the outskirts of Galway town. Since the early Middle Ages, Lydican Castle had been home to the O'Heyne chieftains, who were dispossessed of their lands and castle in the late 17th century when the castle and 1,000 acre estate came into the hands of the Lynch family, in the person of Captain Patrick Lynch. As Patrick Lynch was married to Agnes Blake, it's clear that he was one of the 'tribe' families. It's not clear how the family came into possession of the castle, but suffice to say that they were unlikely to have paid full market value. They took out a large mortgage on the land in 1720, and in later years they relinquished control of the castle as most of their family had emigrated. The Captain's second son, also Patrick, emigrated from Ireland to Spain in the 1740s, and from there he travelled on to Argentina, probably with some family money to help set himself up in South America. In Buenos Aires, Patrick Lynch established himself in Argentinian society, marrying a wealthy heiress called Rosa de Galayn y de la Camara. The family accumulated land while keeping close to their maritime roots and Patrick's grandson Patricio established a shipping company which traded with the United States.

The family grew steadily in wealth and influence. Patricio's son Ventura Lynch inherited a large ranch in the Río de Plata region where Ventura's son Benito and grandson Benito (1882-1951) were raised. The family moved into the town of La Plata, where the older

Benito was director of the newspaper *El Dia*. His son Benito owned shares in and contributed to the same newspaper along with writing short stories and novels. Benito Lynch's novels dealt with the conflict between country labourers and farmhands and the newly arriving European immigrants, and he was admired for his ability to realistically portray the language of the countryside. (In fact, Benito Lynch even earned the attention of the *Great Soviet Encyclopaedia*, which maintained that Lynch created an "authentic and realistic portrayal of the development of capitalist relations in the Argentinian countryside.") Although his novels were turned into plays and films, Lynch failed to appear at any premieres. He avoided the social life of the city and declined literary awards and academic honours. Lynch was a member of the Conservative Party, a distinction he shared with his contemporary Leopoldo Lynch, another journalist and historian.

Despite Benito Lynch's fame, it was another of Patricio Lynch's descendants who would gain the most renown. Patricio's youngest son Francisco was one of Argentina's largest landowners and a colonel in the army. In the late 1840s, when Francisco dared to oppose the Argentinian dictator Juan Manuel de Rosas, he lost his livelihood and his property, and with his son and namesake Francisco he fled to Chile, and then on to California, along with his neighbours, a family of Basque descent called Guevara. They became gold prospectors, but after a unsuccessful stint prospecting, Lynch decided that a steady income could be made selling tools to miners and running a saloon. Lynch married in California and remained there until the 1870s, when he returned to Argentina with his wife and his daughter Ana. The Guevara brothers also returned, and the families later celebrated their reunion when Robert Guevara courted and then married Lynch's daughter Ana. Ernesto Guevara Lynch, the sixth of their eleven children, was born at the turn of the twentieth century.

As Che Guevara's biographer Daniel James notes, Ernesto did not have the adventuring spirit of his forebears, but he married a woman of aristocratic heritage and rebellious spirit. Her name was Celia de la Serna. Bored by city life, the young couple tried their hand at mate farming, and then went into the milling business, settling in the town of Rosaria. It was there that Celia gave birth to her firstborn. Under Spanish and Latin American naming customs, a child may take two surnames, consisting of the father's first surname and the mother's second surname, so although Guevara's father was a Lynch, the boy was known as Ernesto Guevara de la Serna.

By the time Che Guevara was born, the family no longer possessed great riches, but they were far from rebels. In an interview with the writer Iosif Lavretsky, Guevara's father Ernesto Guevara Lynch maintained that Che's radicalism was a genetic affair. He maintained that Che had inherited the restless nature of his Irish ancestors, who had fled Ireland in the 1700s because of their opposition to English dominance. The blood of Irish rebel flowed in Che's veins, said the elder Lynch, and it was this rebel blood that drew Che to dangerous adventures and new ideas. Daniel James, however, writes that the young Ernesto was "essentially his mother's creation", crediting Celia de la Serna for her son's intellectual development and his left-wing ideas. The young Che studied as a doctor, and was radicalised during his travels through South and Central America in the 1950s, becoming involved in Guatemala's socialist government and witnessing the CIA-sponsored coup in 1954. The overthrow of the Arbenz government in Guatemala convinced Guevara of the necessity for armed struggle and when he met up with an exiled Fidel and Raúl Castro in Mexico the following year, he joined the Cuban insurgency. The Cubans gave him the nickname 'Che', from his habit of addressing them as 'che', which roughly translates as *pal* or *mate*. Ernesto Guevara de la Serna became known simply as Che Guevara. The insurgents overthrew the Batista regime in 1959 and installed Castro as the leader of Cuba, with Guevara in charge of training the army and in control of the Cuban forces in the west of the island. Castro and Guevara were sure that the United States would try to overthrow the new regime, just as they had done in Guatemala five years earlier.

The overthrow of Batista was not entirely unpopular in the USA, at least initially, and the Massachusetts Senator John F. Kennedy was pleased to see Batista gone. Castro began nationalising assets and in the febrile Cold War atmosphere the US government under Dwight Eisenhower started to plan a counteroffensive against his regime. Eisenhower's Vice-President Richard Nixon was confident of victory in the 1960 election, and the Republican leadership planned to launch the attack after the election, only to be wrong-footed by the electorate and John F. Kennedy, with assistance from the mob and Kennedy's wily father who reportedly swung the election.

When Kennedy took office in January 1961, the CIA impressed on him the urgency of implementing the Cuban plan. The Kennedy brothers were fascinated by intelligence operations and were great admirers of Ian Fleming and his fictional agent James Bond. According to some accounts, on taking office, John F. Kennedy asked to speak to the CIA's version of James Bond and was disappointed when the CIA brought in their top assassin, a dour man called William Harvey who bore no resemblance to the dapper fictional British spy. The CIA impressed on Kennedy the need for speedy action before the Russians could start reinforcing Castro's army, and Kennedy agreed to a plan that involved mostly Cuban exiles, led by Grayston Lynch and William Robertson, a veteran CIA officer who had helped to overthrow the Arbenz government in Guatemala in 1954. The stage was set for Grayston Lynch and Che Guevara to do battle.

Since April 1960, Lynch and Robertson had been in Miami training the disaffected Cubans who had been leaving the island since the overthrow of Batista in 1959, complaining that Castro's promise of a democratic country had turned sour. Lynch and Robertson's outfit was known as the '2506 Brigade', and the two men were officially to serve as troubleshooters on the mission, though in reality they were in charge of both planning and execution. Most of those recruited to run the operation were Cubans, with the CIA conscious of being able to deny responsibility should anything go wrong. The plan revolved around a simple deception: The CIA would provide US planes painted over with the Cuban flag, and these planes would take out the Cuban air force, giving the impression of an internal revolt. Meanwhile, the Cuban exiles would land a small army on the Cuban coast by boat. Once in Cuba, the rebel force would rouse what the CIA believed was a powerful anti-Castro sentiment, building a significant force that would overwhelm the Cuban army.

The CIA had encountered successes in its coup planning in Iran in 1953, Guatemala in 1954 and Indonesia in 1958, though the coups had not been entirely smooth operations. The CIA-led covert action against Guatemala involved radio propaganda and leaflet drops to convince the population that the coup was being led from inside the army, but when the Guatemalan army defeated the rebel forces in skirmishes, the CIA turned to the US military for reinforcements. A series of air strikes broke the army's resolve, and led to the resignation of Arbenz. Inside the agency, there was confidence that once a covert action was underway in Cuba, the US government would jump in and provide military support rather than countenance defeat. As it turned out, the CIA had gravely overstated the popular appetite for counterrevolution in Cuba, while the White House had gravely overestimated the CIA's chances of success.

The problems began before a single boat was launched. Leaks started to come from the ranks of the hundreds of exiles getting ready to invade Cuba, as word spread around the Cuban community of imminent action against Castro. Word filtered back to Castro, and in national and Miami newspapers, journalists speculated about military action, forcing Kennedy to deny that any invasion was planned. The leaks unnerved the State Department which immediately began to water down the intensity of the operation, ordering that fewer planes be used to cover the Bay of Pigs assault.

On April 15, Lynch and Robertson's invasion force set out from their Nicaraguan base towards Cuba while a smaller than planned squad of B-26 bombers wearing the flag of the Cuba air force left from Nicaragua and attacked three Cuban airfields, taking out a few of the planes on the ground but leaving several intact. After taking fire from the Cubans, one of the disguised B-26s limped back to Miami airport, where the pilots claimed to be defectors. The Cuban ambassador pointed out that the plane was not a Cuban air force plane. On April 16, with Cuba on high alert, Kennedy cancelled further air attacks, in an attempt to retain plausible deniability of US involvement.

Lynch, Robertson and the 1,447 Cubans were already at the Cuban coast, and confusion reigned as they waited for the expected air attacks. Certain that the government would back the military to weigh in once fighting was underway, the boats landed as planned in the pre-dawn darkness of April 17. Lynch made the decision to join the first men landing on the beach, and later admitted that he had fired the first shots when a militia patrol came down to the beach to investigate the lights offshore. It was a reckless move for a CIA man who was supposed to melt into the background of the operation.

The CIA men were sure that Castro was likely to get wind of the operation, and had sent a decoy force towards Pinar Del Rio, 350 miles to the north of the Bay of Pigs. Guevara and his troops raced there only to discover that they had been tricked. When Castro realised that the force was coming ashore at the Bay of Pigs, he sent the remaining troops into action. Without air cover, Lynch's forces were at the mercy of Castro's remaining air force planes. Three days after their arrival on the beachhead, the battle ended in a humiliating defeat for the invaders, with most of the exiled Cubans killed in the fighting or taken prisoner by the Cuban army.

By the time Guevara arrived at the Bay of Pigs, the fighting had finished, leaving Guevara to take control of the prisoners and claim a great victory. Lynch and Robertson escaped back to Washington, where according to Lynch, they discovered that the President himself had cancelled the air raids that would have given cover to their invasion: "This may have been a politically proper way to fight a war, according to the rules laid down by the 'armchair generals' of Camelot", Lynch wrote, "but we called it murder." Lynch raged that Kennedy had failed to stand up to his own State Department, and had pliantly approved request after request from the State Department to water down the invasion plan.

Lynch and Robertson were called before a Pentagon committee that included Robert Kennedy. According to Lynch's account of the investigation, Kennedy was determined to show that the invasion would have failed even without the withdrawal of the air cover. Lynch left the hearings incensed and on May 1, he watched the May Day parade in Cuba with dismay, as newly supplied Russian MiG jets flew over Havana. For the first time in his life, he wrote, he was ashamed of his country. Che Guevara's star rose further on the back of the Cuban victory, and the Cubans trumpeted their ability to defeat the Western superpower. Che Guevara taunted Kennedy, sending him a note that read: "Thanks for Playa Girón. Before the invasion, the revolution was weak. Now it's stronger than ever."

In the US, mainstream media questioned the CIA plan, and reports would appear in the *New York Times* in 1964 that Kennedy had told an administration aide at the time that he planned to break up the agency into "a thousand pieces and scatter it to the wind". In November 1961, Kennedy began the clear out of those he considered most dangerous, getting rid of Allan Dulles, the powerful head of the agency. Yet the agency soon eased its way back into the favour of the White House and redoubled its efforts to overthrow Castro. In late 1961, the CIA established a centre in Miami codenamed JM/WAVE, with the task of killing Castro and overthrowing his regime. Lynch and Robertson were assigned to the Cuban Task Force at JM/WAVE where the assassination group, comprised of government assassins and their underworld counterparts, was named ZR/RIFLE. Robert Kennedy installed the master spies William Harvey and Edward Lansdale at the head of the operation. According to Grayston Lynch, Robert Kennedy took a keen interest in the project, showing up unannounced and on occasion trying to direct operations himself.

Russia continued to upgrade the Cuban military, and tensions continued to escalate, resulting in the Cuban Missile Crisis of 1962 which brought the world to the brink of nuclear war. When the crisis had been resolved, Kennedy moved to change his approach to Cuba and removed Harvey from charge of the assassination team. Kennedy's new appointment Desmond Fitzgerald favoured a more modern approach to the no less unsavoury business of the killing of Castro. The CIA team had not forgotten the perceived betrayal of the Bay of Pigs. "It should be intuitively obvious", wrote Robert Kirkconnell in *American Heart of Darkness*, "that a program to murder other heads of state, and especially ones that are staffed by organised crime members, ex-Nazis, CIA psychopaths and other murderers could be co-opted to blow your head off." The ZR/RIFLE group was manned by several CIA assassins who were deeply hostile to the Kennedy White House, including David Morales and Félix Rodríguez, and mob assassins such as Johnny Roselli. Bradley Ayers, who was seconded from the army to the CIA to work as a paramilitary trainer for JM/WAVE from May 1963 to December 1964, claimed that a group of nine trainers at JM/WAVE including Grayston Lynch had "intimate knowledge" of the JFK assassination.

In the world of spooks and disinformation, it's difficult to take anything at face value but the name of Grayston Lynch appeared often enough in the literature about the Kennedy assassination that later in his life, Lynch was forced to deny that he had anything to do with it, though he did concede that the men he worked with hated Kennedy enough to kill him.

John F. Kennedy was murdered in November 1963, and Vice-President Lyndon B. Johnson replaced him in the Oval Office. Johnson, who was reelected in 1964 and served until 1968, maintained that the Cubans had assassinated Kennedy in revenge for the attempted murder of Castro. With John F. Kennedy out of the picture, the JM/WAVE station continued its mission with the CIA training Cuban exiles in guerrilla warfare and assassination. JM/WAVE became the biggest employer in the Miami area in the mid-1960s, with up to 15,000 Cubans on its payroll. Grayston Lynch ran his own commando group, and by his own admission, ran hundreds of operations against Cuba during the 1960s. These efforts included attempts to plant exploding seashells in Castro's favoured diving spots but Castro somehow survived all efforts to kill him. The station was more successful with its other big target, Che Guevara. Philip Agee, a former CIA officer, wrote that Guevara was the person most feared by the CIA because he possessed the charisma necessary to direct the struggle against the traditional hierarchies that held power in the countries of South America. Like Castro, Guevara proved to be unreachable in Cuba, but once he departed the island, he became an easier target. In one apparent attempt at assassinating Castro, Guillermo Novo fired a bazooka from across the east river at the United Nations during Guevara's address to the UN in 1964, but the shell landed in the water.

In 1965, Che Guevara left Cuba for Africa before travelling to Europe. During a visit from Prague to Cuba, Guevara stopped over in Ireland, at Shannon airport, and spent a day in Limerick city, where he was interviewed by an Irish reporter, Arthur Quinlan, who carved out a niche for himself interviewing various politicians and celebrities who passed through Shannon. Quinlan was alerted to Guevara's arrival by American journalist Bob Loughlin, who according to Quinlan had a "small PR business at the Shannon Development Company". (Quinlan later came to suspect that Loughlin worked for the CIA.) Quinlan knew of Guevara's Lynch ancestry, and though he was told that Guevara spoke no English, he challenged Guevara thus: "Anybody whose maternal grandparents were Lynches either speaks Gaelic or English. Which is it to be?" After visiting Limerick, Guevara met with Bernie Brennan, an Irish-American journalist. "Mr. Brennan had spent much time in Cuba and it was generally believed that he was something of a 'double-agent' who had served the American CIA," wrote Quinlan.

Guevara didn't seem overly impressed to be in the land of his forebears, and may well have been spooked by the various agents hanging about in Shannon. He wrote to his father about his Irish visit: "I am in this green Ireland of *your* ancestors [my italics added]. When they found out, the television came to ask me about the Lynch genealogy, but in case they were horse thieves or something like that, I didn't say much." (Guevara had been interviewed for Irish television in November 1964 during a brief stopover in Dublin airport, so it's not clear which visit he was referring to.) In 1966, Guevara arrived in Bolivia, having decided that South America was the next revolutionary front.

Félix Rodríguez, working for JM/WAVE, was tasked with tracking down Che Guevara and in 1967, the CIA man finally caught up with Che Guevara in the jungle of Bolivia. Rodríguez would later say that he wanted to take Guevara alive, and bring him to Panama for questioning, but the Bolivian President René Barrientos had ordered the execution of the Argentinian revolutionary. Rodríguez oversaw the killing, and took Guevara's watch, which he kept as a memento.

The killing of Guevara turned him into a figurehead for a generation of young people and students across the world. In 1968, the Irish artist Jim Fitzpatrick produced a monochrome drawing of Guevara based on a famous photograph by Alberto Korda, and released it as a copyright–free image. Within weeks, the image was appearing at rallies and protests around the world; not long afterwards, it was appearing on t-shirts. The image is nearly as ubiquitous as the logo of Nike or McDonalds – and indeed, I've seen people wearing a Che Guevara t-shirt while wearing Nikes and eating in McDonalds.

Grayston Lynch left the CIA in 1971 and joined the newly formed Drugs Enforcement Agency (DEA) in Key West, though it's not entirely clear whether the DEA was preventing the flow of drugs or taking part. The end of the JM/WAVE programme had put thousands of Cuban exiles out of work and many of them turned their hand to narcotics smuggling. Cocaine began flooding through the Caribbean island en route to the United States during the 1970s and Miami continued to feature as the headquarters of drug smuggling through the Iran-Contra era, which also featured many of the main players from JM/WAVE. Through the rest of his working life and into his retirement, Lynch maintained a deep hatred of the Kennedys. He was a source for veteran investigative journalist Seymour Hersh's 1997 book *The Dark Side of Camelot*, which somewhat deflated the Kennedy myth. In the book, Hersh noted that the Kennedys were willing to order the assassination of a sovereign head of state.

The year after Hersh's book came out, Lynch published his own account of the Bay of Pigs, called *Decision for Disaster: Betrayal at the Bay of Pigs*. The betrayal in the subtitle referred to the Kennedys. Much of the information, Lynch wrote, was no longer classified, and he stated that the principal reason for doing the book was to put the record straight. He claimed that the true story of the invasion had never been told, and offered his own on-the-ground insights into the failure of the operation. Following the failed invasion, Lynch wrote, he had been involved in the effort to oust Castro, and had waited for someone to step forward and erase the misconceptions that had obscured what he considered to be the facts. Judging that this had not happened, and realising that he was the last remaining American survivor of the Bay of Pigs, he wrote that he felt compelled to record his own account of the events. In the book, Lynch maintained that his account would go some way towards combating the efforts of writers loyal to Kennedy to lay disproportionate blame for the failure on the CIA. *Decision for Disaster* does add new detail to the invasion, though it's largely a savage broadside against those that Lynch considered to be armchair generals. The killing of Kennedy does not earn a mention.

Decision for Disaster initially looked as though it would rewrite history when Ron Howard optioned the book for Universal Studios and Clint Eastwood was approached to play the hero. Yet the project never fell into place, and the option ran out after three years and was never renewed. Instead it was the story of Guevara that hit the movie theatres with the 2004 Spanish-language film *The Motorcycle Diaries*, based on Che Guevara's diary of his 1952 motorcycle trek up through South and Central America. Grayston Lynch planned to write a second book about his continued work against Cuba in the later part of the 1960s but he died in 2008 before completing the book, just as Hollywood was producing its first major movie about Guevara, a two-parter called *Che*, starring Benicio Del Toro and directed by Steven Soderbergh.

Galway played a final cameo in the story of the Lynches of the Bay of Pigs in 2011, when the socialist city councillor Billy Cameron proposed a monument to Che Guevara to commemorate the revolutionary as a 'son of Galway.' The local arts office came up with a mock-up of a monument based on the famous drawing by Jim Fitzpatrick but mutterings soon started that the stern visage of the communist revolutionary would frighten away American tourists. Cuban-born US Congresswoman Ileana Ros-Lehtinen stoked the controversy by writing that the plan was "an insult to all of us who care about the cause of democracy and historical accuracy", although the congresswoman was not to know that historical accuracy was no obstacle to a successful tourist attraction in the City of the Tribes. Shill, the possibility that American tourists would bypass Galway because of the perceived support for Guevara gave cause for concern, and the city council voted against the proposed monument.

No one has yet proposed a Galway monument to that other son of the Lynch tribe and hero of the anti-Castro Cubans, Grayston L. Lynch. Indeed, it may have irritated the old soldier to know that the main plaza of Galway – although colloquially known by its old name Eyre Square – is officially titled the John F. Kennedy Memorial Park.

JACK LYNCH

I was pointedly asked one time by an American historian whether I was a Cork Lynch or a Galway Lynch. I was, I explained, a Lynch from Dublin with Galway roots. The historian looked a bit disappointed. He was, he said, an admirer of Jack Lynch, the "quintessential Corkman". Jack Lynch was one of Ireland's top Gaelic sports stars and was barrister by profession. He entered politics in the 1950s and served twice as the leader of the country in the late 1960s and late 1970s. He's fondly remembered across all political parties as a rather courteous and mellow pipe-smoker who was reluctant to become a politician and leader, and only stepped into the role out of a sense of duty and public service. Yet, few rise to the top in Ireland without some cunning, guile and ruthlessness. In Jack Lynch's case, we can add a good degree of luck and a pointed contrast with his successor Charlie Haughey.

Jack Lynch attended the North Monastery Christian Brothers School in Cork, where he excelled at sports, eventually gaining a place on the Cork county hurling and Gaelic football team. He moved to Dublin in the early 1940s and trained as a barrister, before moving back to Cork to begin a private practice. The Cork hurling team of the 1940s enjoyed a great string of successes, with Lynch as captain. By 1946, he had become a sporting legend by becoming the first player to win six All-Ireland medals in a row, five in hurling and one in football.

Lynch's sporting success made him a target for political parties and in 1948 he agreed to stand for election for Fianna Fáil, and won a seat. Under Eamon de Valera, Lynch first became a cabinet minister in 1957, with the education portfolio. When Sean Lemass became Taoiseach in 1959, Lynch moved to industry and commerce, and later became finance minister. As a minister, Lynch was overshadowed by George Colley and the ambitious Charles Haughey, who formed a great rivalry. When Lemass resigned unexpectedly in 1966, Haughey and Colley faced each other in the leadership challenge. Lemass, aware of the divisions that were likely to emerge in a two-way contest between Haughey and Colley, pushed Lynch forward as a candidate. Lynch's candidacy proved popular and he won the leadership and went on to lead Fianna Fáil to a comfortable victory in the 1969 election.

The late 1960s was marked by student uprisings and revolutions, and a major civil rights movement had started in Northern Ireland in 1968, inspired by events in the USA and elsewhere. On August 12, 1969, the loyalist Apprentice Boys band was allowed to march to the edge of the Bogside, the Catholic area just outside the walls of the old city of Derry, kicking off two days of fighting, and setting off conflicts around the province. In the ensuing unrest, hundreds of nationalist families were forced out of their homes and many fled south across the border seeking refuge.

Jack Lynch returned from his summer holidays and called an emergency cabinet meeting on August 13 and then appeared on television, where he deplored the sectarian nature of the conflict and warned against the involvement of British troops, calling instead for the deployment of a UN peacekeeping force. Speculated was rife that Lynch would send Irish troops into Northern Ireland, though Lynch was a moderate, and had never contrived to use force. Troops were sent to the border, ostensibly to protect field hospitals set up to treat injured northerners.

Lynch's political foes inside his own party didn't agree with the noninterventionist policy. Charles Haughey and the hardline Donegal TD Neil Blaney began working to obtain arms to send to northern Ireland, apparently without Lynch's knowledge. The government had established a civilian relief fund to help nationalist families that had been forced out of their homes during the conflict, and Haughey as minister for finance was in charge of the fund. Blaney and Irish army officer James Kelly arranged for the purchase of weapons from Europe, with Haughey approving the money from the civilian fund. The subsequent string of events have never been fully explained.

The Irish police's special branch got wind of the plot and informed Lynch, who made no moves to intervene. Was Lynch aware of what was happening? It seems likely. Several months later, an anonymous source tipped off opposition leader Liam Cosgrave with the same information, and confronted by Cosgrave, Lynch was forced to act. He confronted Haughey and Blaney, who refused to resign, and were fired. (The sacking of a government minister in Ireland was and still is highly unusual.) Haughey, Blaney and Kelly were put on trial, but the case collapsed, leaving bitter divisions in Fianna Fáil between Lynch's supporters and the more militant supporters of Haughey and Blaney. The ambitious Haughey was effectively banished from the front benches for several years.

Following several years of exile on the back benches during which he toured the country relentlessly, Charles Haughey returned to the cabinet table, and Lynch led the party back into power in 1977 with a huge majority of 20 seats. He stepped down in 1979 and allowed the Haughey-Colley battle to resolve itself with Haughey becoming Taoiseach for the first time, but leading a fractious party that would eventually split five years later with the formation of the Progressive Democrats.

Much of what has written about Jack Lynch suggests that Lynch 'rose without a trace'; that his greatest achievements were the avoidance of disasters; that his preferred method was to react rather than to innovate; and that his manner was to preside over the country without really doing anything. (In retrospect this seems like a rather Taoist approach.) Although Lynch's achievements were less than legion, it may be that the fondness with which he is remembered is more to do with the people who preceded and followed him. Charles Haughey's political career ended in disgrace, so Lynch's rivalry with Haughey elevates Lynch's reputation by default. To put Jack Lynch's work in context, it's worth noting, historically, that his sponsor Seán Lemass was responsible for the establishment of TACA, the fundraising wing of Fianna Fáil that gave builders and industrialists unprecedented and access to the party and its grandees and allowed them unwarranted influence over party policy in the following decades, and Lynch ruled over a party at a time when Fianna Fáil policy catered to the needs of the rising class of Irish industrialists and their multinational counterparts. As the historian D.R. O'Connor Lysaght scathingly observed in a review of Dermot Keogh's biography of Lynch in *History Ireland* magazine, the rich had to pay for Charles Haughey but could rely on Jack Lynch to do what they wanted through his deference and lack of imagination. As party leader, Lynch was the sponsor of Desmond O'Malley, who eventually left Fianna Fáil to establish the Progressive Democrats, a party that enjoyed a period in power before dissolving ignominiously in 2009 after being widely blamed for introducing many of the policies had contributed to the financial crash.

In short, Jack Lynch is remembered as a humble and unprepossessing man who drove a Cork-built Ford at a time when most ministers drove Mercedes. To historians of the Lynch family, Jack represented the humble Gaelic Lynches as opposed to the mercantile power-grabbers of Galway. In his own way though, Jack Lynch was a servant of the modern-day merchants of Ireland.

THE LEGEND OF WILLIE LYNCH

In 1995, the leader of the US-based Nation of Islam Louis Farrakhan organised a Million Man March on Washington DC. The gathering evoked the 'March on Washington for Jobs and Freedom' of August 1963 which culminated in Dr. Martin Luther King's famous call for justice and civil rights, though Farrakhan's plan was to draw attention to the unfulfilled promises of the civil rights movement.

In the course of his speech, Farrakhan referred to a speech, known as the 'How to make a slave' speech that had allegedly been written by a slave owner and delivered to other slaveowners on banks of the James River in 1711, to illustrate how slaveowners had successfully sown hatred and mistrust among the slaves. The letter began with a greeting to the slaveholders of Virginia:

"Gentlemen, I greet you here on the bank of the James River in the year of our Lord one thousand seven hundred and twelve. First, I shall thank you, the gentlemen of the Colony of Virginia, for bringing me here. I am here to help you solve some of your problems with slaves. Your invitation reached me on my modest plantation in the West Indies where I have experimented with some of the newest and still the oldest methods of control of slaves. Ancient Rome would envy us if my program were implemented. As our boat sailed south on the James River, named for our illustrious King, whose version of the Bible we cherish, I saw enough to know that your problem is not

118

unique. While Rome used cords of woods as crosses for standing human bodies along its highways in great numbers you are here using the tree and the rope on occasion. I caught the whiff of a dead slave hanging from a tree a couple of miles back. You are not only losing a valuable stock by hangings, you are having uprisings, slaves are running away, your crops are sometimes left in the fields too long for maximum profit, you suffer occasional fires, your animals are killed. Gentlemen, you know what your problems are: I do not need to elaborate. I am not here to enumerate your problems, I am here to introduce you to a method of solving them. In my bag here, I have a fool proof method for controlling your Black slaves. I guarantee everyone of you that if installed correctly it will control the slaves for at least 300 hundred years [sic]. My method is simple. Any member of your family or your overseer can use it."

Louis Farrakhan proceeded to the portion of the speech that taught slaveowners how to maintain disharmony among the ranks of the slaves:

"You must use the female against the male. And you must use the male against the female. You must use the dark skinned slaves against the white skinned slaves. And the light skinned slave against the dark skinned slave. You must also have your white servants and overseers distrust all blacks. Gentlemen, these are your keys to control. Use them. Never miss an opportunity. And if used intensely for one year, the slaves themselves will remain perpetually distrustful. Thank you, gentlemen."

Farrakhan concluded: "So spoke Willie Lynch 283 years ago." The speech, which was broadcast live on the cable channel CSPAN, introduced many viewers to 'Willie Lynch'. The nearly 300-year-old 'Willie Lynch letter' became a phenomenon among black Americans, so accurately did it appear to describe the myriad injustices and internalisation of hatred suffered by black Americans. Historians and journalists began to dig into the origins of the speech, which appeared to have been posted online by a librarian at a university in St. Louis. The librarian had culled the speech from the pages of the *St. Louis Black Pages* in 1993; the publisher of the *Black Pages* had taken the speech from a photocopied document that appeared to have circulated in the black community since 1970.

Some scholars noted cautiously that the language of Willie Lynch's speech was uncannily modern. Manu Ampin, an historian of African affairs, challenged the authenticity of the letter and suggested that William Lynch was a fictional character. Ampin gave several reasons. His main contention was that the William Lynch speech had escaped the attention of every slavemaster and anti-slavery activist of the 18th and 19th century, along with historians of slavery. He maintained that the only known William Lynch was born in 1742, and that aspects of Lynch's speech were full of idiosyncrasies that belonged to the 20th century.

In 2007, the American writer Rahim Muhammad published *Willie Lynch: Real of Imaginary*, challenging Ampin's assumptions. Undertaking some basic research, Muhammad had discovered that there was indeed a William Lynch living in Barbados in 1715 and another William Lynch resident in Antigua in 1727. Muhammad's research of the Lynch families in the Caribbean was enough to convince him that the Lynches were indeed part of the Caribbean elite. The Lynches, wrote Muhammad, clearly owned a lot of slaves and passed them on to their descendants. Muhammad went on to conclude that William Lynch was in fact the son of Thomas Lynch, the English Governor of Jamaica who died in 1684. Further documents uncovered by Muhammad showed that there was indeed significant commerce, traffic and interaction between Barbados and the other Caribbean islands and the colony of Virginia.

Muhammad's research purported that the Willie Lynch letter was within the realms of possibility. Ampin, he suggested, was wrong to write off the possibility that there had been a real William Lynch.

There was one more twist to the story. In 2013, Dr. Kwabena Ashanti, a psychology lecturer from North Carolina, admitted to Manu Ampin that he was the author of the Willie Lynch document. He had written the document in 1970, he said, to present his theories about the divisions inherent in 20th century black communities. In coming up with a villain of the piece, Dr. Ashanti had chosen well. Although Ashanti had made up the historical details and geographical details, they did have a basis in reality. The fact that so many people accepted the document as truthful did not prove its readers to be gullible; rather it showed that Dr. Ashanti's piece had more than a ring of truth to it, and was solidly grounded in American mythology.

When we consider the family of Charles Lynch, who gave the world Lynch law, we can easily imagine the events that may have inspired Ashanti's story. Although Lynch arrived from Ireland in 1718 or later (and therefore too late to be the person in question), he did marry into the Clark family, who themselves had been slaveowners and landowners in Barbados before buying land in Virginia around 1705. Ashanti, it appears, had expertly blended together the stories associated with the name Lynch to come up with a horror story that cut all too close to the bone.

THE STARS OF LYNCH

The fact that the most famed Lynches of the 21st century are not merchants or mayors but entertainers and celebrities perhaps says more about modern society than it does about the extended Lynch tribe. Celebrity culture may appear pervasive today in the information age when public celebrities document their daily lives through tweets and 'selfies' but it's been around since the the origins of the popular press in the 18th century.

Celebrity culture has long been a driver of the business of selling newspapers and magazines. It's said that 'newspaper never refuses ink' and with the growing demand for newspapers and magazines two hundred years ago, editors and reporters sought out figures whose exploits could regularly sell out editions. Jockeys, boxers, actors and comedians featured regularly as did women from high and low society who could impress the public with their grasp of style and fashion. The press gave criminals a degree of notoriety previously available to only the most prolific thieves and murderers. With each new medium, from radio to cinema to television and the internet, celebrities have enjoyed increased channels of access to the public to the extent that celebrities are now defined by their reach and appeal. Loosely defined, we could say that celebrity culture is a business relationship as popular public figures gain wealth and influence in exchange for sharing the intimate details of their lives with the general public.

Shane Lynch: So who are the Lynch stars of modern times? In Ireland, the family of Shane Lynch and his sisters Edele and Keavy feature prominently in the celebrity stakes. Shane Lynch was among the five young men selected by impresario Louis Walsh to form the Irish boyband Boyzone, delivering an Irish version of the successful English act Take That. Contrary to the much cherished opinion that popular culture has fallen to bits with the advent of manufactured pop groups, it's worth noting that 'manufactured' pop groups are nothing new. Even Bob Marley's early trio of Wailers alongside Peter Tosh and Bunny Livingston, celebrated for their rootsy and authentic sound, competed in talent shows in Kingston before going on to bigger things. Let's just say that the manufacturing process became more sophisticated. The 1990s boy and girl band phenomenon produced celebrity-ready bands, with each member assigned a role designed to appeal to different demographics among their following. The Spice Girls famously played on this idea, giving us 'Posh' Spice, 'Sporty Spice', 'Scary Spice', 'Baby Spice' and 'Ginger Spice'.

Shane Lynch played the nonconformist member of Boyzone, with his tattoos, piercings and general bad boy image contrasting with the clean cut look of the other four members. Although Boyzone never broke into the American market, they sold millions of albums and singles in the UK market before breaking up at the turn of the millennium. Over the following years Shane Lynch acted in television shows and on stage and took part in several reality television shows that lean towards celebrity participants. Lynch became a born-again Christian in 2006 and wrote about his experiences in his autobiography *The Chancer*.

His sisters, twins Edele and Keavy, formed the pop group B*Witched with Lindsay Armanou and Sinéad O'Carroll, and went on to have a successful five-year career, selling several million albums. When the band was dropped by its label and split, the twin sisters formed a band called Ms Lynch. In 2013, Edele won Celebrity

Apprentice Ireland, while Shane came in fifth place on Celebrity Masterchef.

Lynch: Not being born under the name Lynch has proved no obstacle for several diverse singers and bands. Take for instance the band simply named lynch (which is written in a lower-case fraktur font), which is a Japanese kei metal band established in 2004 in Nagoya, Japan. Nagoya kei metal is a genre of Japanese heavy metal influenced by punk and Western goth music and sensibilities: Think young, moody-looking Japanese dressed in black. Their 2014 album is called *Gallows*.

Lynch Mob: One name that has proved irresistible for bands is the Lynch mob, though even attempts at ironic usage are perhaps ill-advised in light of its historical use to describe racially-motivated murdering gangs. George Lynch was the guitarist of 1980s group Dokken, a hugely successful 'hair metal' band that sold more than 10 million albums before breaking up in the late 1980s. In 1989 George Lynch formed Lynch Mob as a hard rock band outfit which went through several members over the next decades, with Lynch the only permanent member. The band broke up and reformed several times, trying various directions including an attempt at rap metal which had been popularized by bands such as Limp Bizkit. Lynch apparently referred to this period as 'Lynch Bizkit.' Lynch Mob continues to periodically reform and dissolve.

Da Lench Mob: While it's possible that George Lynch's Lynch Mob have black fans, they're probably few in number, as hard rock never gained much of a following with black audiences. The early days of West Coast rap in the late 1980s and early 1990s did however give birth to Da Lench Mob. The odd spelling was deliberate: As one fan explained, 'proper spelling is for crackers' i.e. white people, and as Da Lench Mob was a black group, their use of the concept was most certainly an appropriation of the concept rather than an unwitting use. Da Lench Mob staked their claim to fame in the early 1990s with a series of songs that teetered on the edge of outright racism. It takes no great leap of the imagination to see that Da Lench Mob were lyrically turning the tables on institutional racism and centuries of anti-black violence. In the song 'Environmental Terrorist', Da Lench Mob state their intention to 'Lynch a thousand a week if it's necessary'.

So it was that the name 'Lench' got a revival, eight centuries after some of the first Lynch families to arrive in Ireland took the same name, albeit as 'De Lench' rather than 'Da Lench'. The name Da Lench Mob is of course a play on 'lynch mob'. Formed in Los Angeles in the late 1980s, the members of Da Lench Mob were Shorty, J-Dee and T-Bone, and their big break came when they featured on the first solo album of rapper Ice Cube. Ice Cube had become a star with the seminal rap group NWA, which included Dr. Dre and Eazy-E, but left to record his own album with East Coast producers The Bomb Squad. That album, *Amerikkka's Most Wanted*, became a commercial and critical success, pointing to the simmering violence of south central LA that would explode two years later in the LA riots.

The members of Da Lench Mob were surprised to discover that Ice Cube himself was a well-educated middle class boy whose outfits and permanent scowl had convinced all those around him that he was in fact a gangster. Da Lench Mob themselves were genuine gangbangers and their appearance on tour with Ice Cube further convinced onlookers of Ice Cube's gangland credentials. On tour, while Ice Cube kept to the safety of his hotel room, J-Dee and Shorty ventured out into local neighbourhoods to hang out with the ghetto dwellers. "This is something I grew up with all my life," Shorty told an interviewer. "Hanging around cutthroats and weed smokers and heroin addicts, alcoholics. This is all we knew."

Ice Cube continued to support the careers of Da Lench Mob and produced their brilliantly named gold-selling 1992 debut album *Guerrillas in the Mist*. Da Lench Mob, influenced by members of Public Enemy that they had met on tour, turned towards the Nation of Islam. Da Lench Mob's lyrics often used the more sordid aspects of Nation of Islam thinking: they regard themselves as 'top ranking honky killers' who are going to kill 'evil fucking crackers', promising to fill the morgues with 'Caucasian John Does' or 'sending them back on a ship to Europe … they deserve it.'

Rap music in the early 1990s was drawn into an often overwrought 'battle' between East and West Coast groups, though in reality much of the violence derived from feuds between local gangs. While Ice Cube was doing business and building himself a reputation in the broader music world that included film appearances, Da Lench Mob's J-Dee was arrested and convicted of attempted murder. The group hired another rapper called Maulkie and released the album *Planet Of Da Apes* in 1994 but broke up soon afterwards. Ice Cube held on to the name Lench Mob records, and revived it in 2006, releasing his own albums and latterly his son's music.

Lynched: It's not everyone can put together a band called Lynched and not raise eyebrows. Some people argue that there's been an unfilled hole in the Irish musical tradition since the 1970s heyday of the Horslips and their blend of rock and traditional music, though Galway's Big Bag of Sticks did carry the flame for a while during the 1990s, substituting reggae for rock. More recently, it's Dublin band Lynched, composed of Lynch brothers Ian and Daragh (who doubles as illustrator for Dublin magazine *rabble*), Cormac Mac Diarmada and Riada Peat, who have taken up the mantle for folk music from Ireland to the Appalachians in the West and Russia in the east. Along with playing traditional tunes, the group write their own music including a song called 'Cold Old Fire' that describes their feelings of the struggle to survive in Dublin during the austerity years. When offered a gig on the RTÉ (Irish national television) stage during Culture Night 2014, the band were requested to play three songs that did not include 'Cold Old Night' as part of their set. Rather than bowing to censorship, the group decided to press ahead with their plan to play one self-penned song, and apparently by mutual consent were removed from the RTÉ programme. Lynched?

LYNCH ON SCREEN

Jack Nicholson: Okay, so what the heck is Jack Nicholson doing here? Although the name Nicholson has both English and German origins, it turns out that actor Jack Nicholson has strong connections to Ireland, and to the Lynch family. Annoyingly for the Lynch clan, Jack Nicholson's name will forever be associated with the Murphy family following his Oscar-winning performance as Randle Patrick McMurphy in the film of Ken Kesey's book *One Flew Over The Cuckoo's Nest*.

Nicholson grew up in Neptune City in New Jersey and was raised by John Joseph Nicholson and his wife Ethel May, believing them to be his parents. He also believed that June Nicholson was his sister, but in fact she was his mother and John Joseph and Ethel were his maternal grandparents. He didn't realize this until he was in his late 30s, when they were all dead. The identity of Nicholson's father is unknown.

Jack Nicholson's family identified themselves as Catholic Irish, even though his grandmother Ethel May Rhoads came from a Dutch Protestant family who were less than happy that their daughter married a Catholic. Her husband John Joseph Nicholson was the son of Ella Lynch, the daughter of immigrant Irish farmer Timothy Lynch. US census lists record that Ella Lynch was born in Cork in 1866 and arrived in the US in 1880 or 1881, living at first in Orleans, New York and then moving to New Jersey, where she met and married Joseph Nicholson. He was the son of Irishwoman Bridget

Derrig of Mayo and Scottish shoemaker Joseph Nicholson, who married in Kent in England in 1854. Their only child was John Nicholson. Joseph Nicholson died in 1904 and Ella Nicholson raised John alone, which may explain Jack Nicholson's particular love of Ireland: the man he regarded as his father had been brought up by an Irishwoman. (In the Nicholson biography *Jack's Life: A Biography of Jack Nicholson*, author Patrick McGilligan suggests that Ella and Joseph Nicholson may have adopted their only child John.)

Through his childhood, Jack Nicholson was well aware of his Irish origins, and in a roundabout way he came to regard himself as Irish. His long-term partner Angelica Huston spent much of her childhood in Galway, as her film director father John Huston owned St. Cleran's House in Craughwell, and Jack Nicholson visited Galway a number of times with Huston.

On one visit to Ireland in 2008, he spoke to the *Irish Times*, and explained that he came from the Lynches of Sligo, suggesting that he had investigated his Irish roots: "You know, I went there and I looked in the phone book and there are nine million Lynches in Sligo." While this is a slight exaggeration, it did cause many Lynches to smile at the revelation, and welcome a defection from the (Mac)Murphy clan to the Lynches. In one of his later films, Nicholson reprised his Irish-American character acting when he played Irish gangster Francis 'Frank' Costello in the 2006 Martin Scorsese film *The Departed*.

Joe Lynch: Although he enjoyed a wide-ranging career on stage and in television, the Irish actor Joe Lynch will always be remembered for his role in *Glenroe*, the long–running Irish soap opera. He was born in Cork in 1925 and began working at the Irish national radio station Radio Éireann in the late 1940s, where he was a founding member of the repertory company Radio Éireann Players, and by the 1950s he had his own show called *Living With Lynch* which went out on

Sunday evenings.

Through the late 1960s and 1970s he appeared on British soap operas including a spell on Coronation Street but in the late 1970s he returned to Ireland and began a long run on *Bracken*, the rural soap opera that was a spin-off from *The Riordans*. *The Riordans*, which started broadcasting in 1965, was itself a pioneering soap opera. Although soap operas were a staple of early television broadcasters, they were invariably located in urban settings. Recognising that Ireland of the 1960s was still largely rural, Telefís Éireann produced the new show using the outside broadcast unit to film on location. The show ran until 1979, when it was spun off into the series *Bracken* through the character of Pat Barry, played by the young Gabriel Byrne.

Bracken introduced Irish viewers to Dinny Byrne and his son Miley, played by Joe Lynch and Mick Lally. The writer of *Bracken* Wesley Burrowes based the characters on a real father and son, recalling that the father was a simple man while the son was a 'cute hoor' (an Irish expression for a rogue, sometimes but not always lovable). Burrowes reversed the characterisations to brilliant dramatic and comic effect. *Bracken* ran for four years and spun off into the semi-rural soap *Glenroe*, set in a small country village and starring Dinny and his son Miley, and revolving around Miley's relationship with Biddy McDermott, the daughter of the local solicitor. Mick Lally's character Miley was permanently bamboozled. His expression 'Well, Holy God' became a catchphrase that outlived the actor. Joe Lynch's character Dinny was always on the lookout for quick moneymaking schemes, all the while maintaining an air of bonhomie and chivalry. Fittingly, Dinny's character had his peak during the era that Charlie Haughey was Taoiseach (Prime Minister of Ireland). An Irish joke ran: What's the difference between Charles Haughey and an Aran jumper? The answer: One's a country craft.

Although he had created Lynch's character, Burrowes later

lamented that Joe Lynch would be remembered for his 18 years playing the character of Dinny Byrne. Beyond his acting career, said Burrowes, Joe Lynch had many other talents. He had been a fine boxer and footballer, along with being a talented flautist and singer, and a fine dancer.

Richard Lynch: Few stories are complete without a villain and Richard Lynch was one of the best-known villains in Hollywood. Born in Brooklyn in 1940 to Irish-American parents, he served in the Marine Corps and then began working in theatre. In the course of an LSD trip in New York's Central Park in the summer of 1967, he set himself on fire and almost burned himself to death. He underwent massive reconstructive surgery but was left with permanent scarring on his face. The following year, while recovering from massive reconstructive surgery, he told a documentary film maker: "I was a prosperous, promising young actor. If you had ever told me that I would go to Central Park and try to burn myself to death, I would have said you were out of your mind."

Though badly scarred, Lynch returned to acting although the visible facial scarring led to him being cast as a villain. His first big role came in 1973 alongside Al Pacino and Gene Hoffman in *Scarecrow*, where Lynch played a violent prisoner. He appeared in several TV shows and B-movies as crooked cops and villains, and appeared in cult movies such as *Aztec Mummy* and the 2007 remake of *Halloween*.

IT'S LYNCHIAN

After several hundred years of the word Lynch being used to refer to extrajudicial killing, one man inspired a new concept: Lynchian. That man is American filmmaker and artist David Lynch. The late writer David Foster Wallace suggested that an academic definition of Lynchian might refer to an ironic combination of the macabre and the mundane. By way of explanation, Foster Wallace suggested that an incident in Boston where a deacon was cut off in traffic by another driver and then chased down the culprit and shot him with a crossbow was 'borderline Lynchian'. Another wag suggested this definition of Lynchian was a situation where you have 'no fucking clue what's going on, but you know it's genius'.

For several decades David Lynch has been the best-known Lynch in America, distinguished from other filmmakers by the consistently surrealist bent of his work. Lynch's work tends towards the nightmarish, dystopian and baffling aspects of life, born of his perception that a veneer of banality concealed grotesque realities. David Lynch was born in 1946 in Missoula, Montana but spent his childhood in several states as his father's work with the forestry service required the family to move around and Lynch grew up in several small towns in 1950s America. In US culture, the 1950s has become a shorthand for a stable, prosperous postwar period; it conjures up images of suburban living and white picket fences. In contrast, the 1960s stands for the rejection of a conformist, conservative society but in reality this is simply a convenient manner of arranging historical events. The 1950s were also a time of great turmoil, displacement and re-arrangement, and as other writers have noted, the image of white picket fence 1950s America was largely invented by Hollywood. The young David Lynch noted that beneath the idyllic image of the postwar years lay all of the cultural tension that would explode into public consciousness in the following decades. In one famous quote, he explained that as a child, he observed the surface of middle America as a perfect place of neat gardens and cherry trees: "But then on this cherry tree would be this pitch oozing out, some if it black, some of it yellow, and there were millions and millions of red ants racing all over the sticky pitch, all over the tree. So you see, there's this beautiful world and you look a little bit closer and it's all red ants."

Lynch initially planned a career as a painter, but during his studies in the Pennsylvania Academy of Fine Arts in the mid-1960s he was drawn towards filmmaking and produced a short animated film titled *Six Men Getting Sick* that looped six vomiting characters that bear a resemblance to figures from a Francis Bacon painting. (Lynch later stated that Bacon was his favourite painter.) That short film earned Lynch a commission from H. Barton Wasserman to make the film *The Alphabet*, which in turn earned the support of the American Film Institute. The AFI supported the making of Lynch's debut 1977 feature film *Eraserhead*, a baffling and nightmarish take on family life. *Eraserhead* went on to gain cult status and garnered the attention of Mel Brooks who hired Lynch to direct *The Elephant Man*. That story of a badly deformed man living in 19th century London was nominated for eight Academy Awards and earned Lynch the attention of a wider public.

During the 1980s, Lynch directed two movies that are memorable for different reasons. The first was *Dune*, based on the bestselling dystopian science fiction novel by Frank Herbert. With its air of ecological foreboding, *Dune* was very much of its time, but

Herbert had elected to leave robots and computers out of his future and instead elected to play on more timeless ideas of feudalism. The book was first optioned in 1971 and the producers initially approached David Lean, who turned down the offer. A French consortium then bought the rights and hired maverick director of psychedelic opuses Alexander Jodorowsky. Jodorowsky envisaged a ten-hour epic with Salvador Dalí cast as the Emperor, and Pink Floyd producing the soundtrack. Jodorowsky's production script ran to 14 hours and was the size of a phone book, and millions of dollars were spent in pre-production but the general 1970s-era excess overwhelmed the project. (The special effects director Dan O'Bannon ended up in a psychiatric hospital, though later recovered and produced the script for *Alien*.) The rights for *Dune* then went to the de Laurentiis brothers, who hired Ridley Scott, though Scott dropped out of the project in favour of *Blade Runner*, and later directed *Alien*, making Jodorowsky's failed project a seedbed for *Alien*.

Dino de Laurentiis then hired David Lynch to direct *Dune*. Between publication of the novel in 1965 and the eventual release of the film in 1984, the Star Wars trilogy had become a massive success, drawing on themes similar to those in *Dune* but giving its story cuddly heroes and an easy to grasp narrative. Science fiction fans eagerly awaited *Dune*, but critics greeted the movie with dismay, even though Lynch's penchant for the surreal and alien would have been obvious to viewers of his previous work. Although it's earned a degree of retrospective admiration, *Dune* was panned by critics when it first came out. Lynch later admitted that he did not have control over the final shape of the film, and it almost put paid to his career.

Dune marked the first collaboration between Lynch and the musician Brian Eno, with Eno composing 'Prophecy Theme'. Oddly, the rest of the soundtrack was composed and performed by the rock band Toto, although Eno was rumoured to have previously written and composed an entire score for *Dune*. It's instructive to compare the careers of Lynch and Eno, who were born within a couple of years on one another. Both men trained initially as painters and went on to experiment widely with sound and both independently experimented with looping and reverse recordings to create atmospheric sonic landscapes. It's the close attention to the sonic components and ambient detailing of his visual work that distinguishes much of Lynch's work.

The movie's producer Dino de Laurentiis had contracted Lynch for another movie, which became *Blue Velvet*. It has come to be regarded as rather middle of the road by Lynch's own standards although the violence and sexual content in the script had frightened off other producers. *Blue Velvet* resurrected the career of Dennis Hopper and is now widely regarded by the general public as Lynch's signature movie.

Presaging the current trend for high-end television drama, Lynch moved from the big screen to the small screen with the TV series *Twin Peaks*, which aired from 1990 to 1991 and had a huge cultural impact in the US and abroad. In the show, an FBI agent arrives into the town of Twin Peaks to investigate the murder of homecoming queen Laura Palmer. (In the US, the homecoming queen is the high school student elected to preside over the events surrounding the 'Homecoming' football game, which unites new and former students of the high school.) The premise of *Twin Peaks*, at one level, is that all kinds of phobias and weirdness lie under the superficial normality of a small American town. With its deliberately obscure plot line and refusal to deliver the answer to the question of 'Who killed Laura Palmer', *Twin Peaks* became a talking point as viewers tried to guess the outcome. It anticipated by at least a decade series such as *Lost*, and when network executives successfully prevailed upon the producers to deliver some kind of explanation for the mysteries at the heart of the show, the viewership plunged.

While making *Twin Peaks*, Lynch directed the road movie *Wild At*

Heart which divided critics but won the Palme D'Or at the Cannes Film Festival. Lynch attempted to make another TV series but the studios backed out and he turned the idea into the 2001 movie *Mulholland Drive*, which critics acclaim as one of his best works. During his career as a director, Lynch also designed furniture, exhibited his own art and photography and produced a series of cartoons for the *LA Reader*.

Lynch has released a number of singles and albums including two dance music singles on UK label Sunday Best. He maintains his own website as an outlet for his various productions, including the cartoon *Dumbland*. For several years he used the website to deliver a regular weather report from Los Angeles and the site keeps changing according to his newest or latest project. Fittingly for a man devoted to bringing buried mental landscapes to the surface, he raises money for buildings devoted to housing people practicing transcendental meditation.

LYNCH ON THE FIELD

He drives a Lamborghini sports car, is fond of Skittles, and has a dish named after him at Seattle's CenturyLink sports ground. The Lynchburger is served with a side of Skittles in honour of Marshawn Lynch, the running back who plays for the Seattle Seahawks, who won their first Superbowl in 2014. For many years Jack Lynch was the most famous athlete of the Lynch name, but it's time to retire Jack and hand the honour over to Marshawn.

Marshawn Lynch grew up in a black family in Oakland, California and began playing football at Oakland Technical High School. His mother Delisa Lynch was a high school athlete, and his uncle Lorenzo Lynch had enjoyed an 11-year career in the NFL. At football practice one day, Marshawn's grandfather Loren Lynch encouraged the high school coach to take the boy off the line back and give him a chance to run. Marshawn Lynch became a college football star at the University of California, Berkeley and in 2007 he was drafted by the Buffalo Bills. He joined the Seattle Seahawks in 2010. He was involved in several off-field incidents including an alleged hit-and-run that injured a pedestrian, and possession of a weapon in a separate incident. Though happy to talk to the press for several years, in 2012 Lynch developed a marked reluctance to say more than the necessary minimum. His mother Delisa Lynch explained to the *Seattle Times* that her son stopped talking to the press because of his belief that they "turn everything around."

He was initially fined $50,000 during the 2013 season for his refusal to speak, though Seahawks fans rallied around to pay the fine, which was subsequently rowed back. He declined an invitation to the White House, where President Barack Obama jokingly regretted his absence: "I'm sorry Marshawn is not here because I appreciate his approach to the press – and I want to get some tips from him."

From the time his mother bribed him with Skittles as a child, he developed a taste for the sweets, explaining that they settle his stomach. His consumption of Skittles became a comedy point with fans throwing Skittles onto the field when he earned a score. He was fined for wearing Skittles-coloured studs on his football boots, but Skittles eventually stepped in and offered him a commercial endorsement deal. Lynch's on-field demeanour and focus has been dubbed 'Beast Mode' and Lynch has embraced the term, launching his own Beast Mode clothing brand. Along with Joshua Johnson, a fellow student at Oakland Technical High School, Lynch runs a foundation called Fam 1st Family Foundation to help underprivileged children in the San Francisco Bay area.

THE GEOGRAPHY OF LYNCH

The name Lynch may have originated from Linz, but other places also lay claim to association with the name, as either a place of origin or descent. The Lynch families of England are quite likely to be of a different origin than that Gaelic Lynches and the Anglo-Norman Lynches, for the Lynches of England take their name from Linch, which in turn derives from the old English word *hlinc*, meaning a hillside. (There is a hamlet in Somerset called Lynch, and a hamlet called Linch in West Sussex. Linch records indicate that the parish was never heavily populated; it had 6 inhabitants plus the rector in 1428.)

English records show one Geoffrey Linch appearing as a court witness in Suffolk in 1228, and Gilbert de la Lynch appears in the Subsidy Rolls of Worcestershire in 1275. The best-known of the English Lynch family was Thomas Lynch, who served as Governor of Jamaica on three separate occasions during the 17th century.

Lynchburg, Virginia is the largest 'Lynch' town or city in the world, and dates from the mid-18th century. It's inaccurate to say that Virginia was 'settled' and the word 'planted' or occupied is more accurate, as the arrival of the Europeans forced native Americans out of the area. From the turn of the 17th century, Virginia witnessed a great influx of Scotch-Irish Presbyterians fleeing religious persecution in Ulster, and a wave of Irish immigrants arrived, some directly from Ireland and other from the Caribbean. As we've already seen, many Lynch families had colonised the Caribbean islands, but with the great fortunes to be made from the sugar trade pushing up land prices, many Irish had moved on from places like Barbados and Jamaica, and began to establish themselves in the English colonies of Virginia. However, Lynchburg of Virginia was born of a marriage between an Irish and English family.

The Clark family arrived to Virginia in the late 17th century, after settling first in Barbados, where the name of Christopher Clark and his siblings are listed as land and slave owners in 1680. In Virginia, Christopher Clark purchased land at Cedar Creek in Hanover County. Christopher Clark's son, also Christopher,

One of those arrivals was Charles Lynch from Galway. We've already established that his first son Charles went on to invent 'Lynch law', but his second son John Lynch inherited the land along the banks of the James river. With the growth in plantations, the town of New London had become an important trading centre, but was not easily accessible from northern towns due to the need to ford the James river. According to descendants of the Lynch and Clark families, Charles Lynch was granted permission to keep a ferry between his land and the other side of the river. It's also recorded that it was his son John Lynch who set up the ferry service in 1757. In any case, the landing area for Lynch's Ferry developed into a village, and itself became a centre of trade.

In 1784, John Lynch petitioned the Virginia General Assembly for a charter, which was duly granted in 1786, establishing the town of Lynchburg, and in 1812 Lynch built a bridge to replace the ferry service. From that era, we have some interesting quotes. Thomas Jefferson maintained a home in Poplar Forest close to Lynchburg and considered it "the most interesting spot in the state". He alluded to the rise of commerce, and by 1810 he ranked Lynchburg as the "most rising place in the US" which ranked "next to Richmond in importance". Evangelist Lorenzo Dow was less than impressed with the town. After speaking there, he wrote that he had spoken "in the open air in what I conceived to be the seat of Satan's Kingdom. Lynchburg was a deadly place for the worship of God". Lynchburg was a commercially successfully town, and by the outbreak of the civil war, it was the second wealthiest city per capita after the whaling town of New Bedford in Massachusetts. As a centre of tobacco growing, Lynchburg contributed a novel invention to the world in 1880, when local resident James Albert Bonsack produced the world's first cigarette rolling machine, which revolutionised the industry.

While Lynchburg, Virginia (pop. 75,568) became closely associated with the vice of tobacco, its namesake 500 miles to the southwest would become famous for another vice. Lynchburg, Tennessee (pop. 6,339) is one of those places that produced an odd combination of an Irish and German name ('burg' from Old German, for a fortified town). The town's most famous resident was not a Lynch, but Jack Daniel, who founded the distillery that's home to the world's best-selling whiskey.

Lynchburg was first settled around 1800, but the origin of the town's name is not clear. As is often the case, there are several explanations. The oldest (and probably most accurate) reference is from an 1876 article in the *Lynchburg Sentinel* which suggests the town was named after its Virginia namesake. A Depression-era WPA Guide from 1935 suggests that the town was founded by Tom Lynch. An article in the *Tennessee Historical Quarterly* from 1972 comes up with the old favourite that the town was named for a 'Judge Lynch' who ran a vigilante committee. As we know, it was indeed Charles Lynch of the Lynches of Lynchburg, Virginia who became famous as the instigator of Lynch law; the *Tennessee Historical Quarterly* article is an example of historical fact winding back on itself. There are other Lynchburgs: there is a Lynchburg in Ohio (pop. 1,499) and a Lynchburg, South Carolina (pop. 359).

There's a Lynch county in Maryland, and there are towns called Lynch in Nebraska (pop. 238) and Kentucky (pop. 726). The town of

Lynch, Kentucky lies in the southeastern corner of Harlan County, high in the Appalachian mountains. Lynch was a company town, built expressly for the purpose of housing workers for the coal mine. Set at an altitude of 523m, it was laid out in 1917 for the US Coal and Coke Company (which later became a subsidiary of US Steel), and was the biggest coal camp in the world at the time. It was named after Thomas Lynch, who had been the first president of the company from 1897 until 1914. As Appalachian lawyer told the oral historian Alessandro Portelli in the book *They Say In Harlan County: An Oral History*, the town was an example of advanced corporate paternalism. With enough coal at the nearby mine to last a generation, the town of Lynch was built to last, with high-quality housing and well laid out streets, parks and conveniences. The public buildings were cut from sandstone, and with running water and electricity in each house, the town was a far cry from the makeshift nature of most coal camps.

The company had to provide good conditions in order to attract workers. Locals worked on the construction but declined to take the tough mining jobs, so the company recruited Hungarians, Poles, Irish, Mexicans, Italians and African-Americans to run the mines. Lynch combined elements of a well-run company town and the chaos of a frontier town. With shifts working around the clock, the mine soon became the largest producer of coal in the world, and in 1923, the workers mined 12,820 tons of coal in a single nine-hour shift. Residents recalled that the town was alive 24 hours a day, with a card game or a party always going on somewhere. At its peak, Lynch had 10,000 residents, all connected with the mines, with the company controlling all aspects of daily life. It employed its own police force to keep union organisers out of the town and to intimidate any miners that tried to join a union.

Harlan County was the site of many protests and confrontations between the United Mine Workers Association and the coal companies and despite the anti-union sentiment, Lynch was one of the best of the company towns. Thirty miles to the southwest, the workers at Duke Power Company's Brookside Mine toiled under dreadful conditions. When the UMWA organised a strike against the Duke Power Company in 1972, the filmmaker and labour activist Barbara Kopple arrived and spent the following years documenting the confrontation. Her film *Harlan County, USA* won an Oscar for Best Documentary in the 1977 Academy Awards and shone a light on a corner of the USA that rarely made the news. Today, the mines above Lynch are closed and less than 1,000 people live in the town. In Lynch, Mine Portal 31 serves as Kentucky's 'first exhibition coal mine'.

SAVING PRIVATE LYNCH

The story of Jessica Lynch was, at first sight, remarkable. The young American woman from a poor Appalachian community had joined the US army to broaden her horizons and secure her college education, only to find herself throw into the front lines of the invasion of Iraq. Private Jessica Lynch was captured in an ambush in the early days of the invasion of Iraq in March 2003 and despite being shot, she fought bravely until she ran out of ammunition. Reports told how she was tortured and raped by Iraqi militia forces for several days until a brave Iraqi lawyer risked his life to reveal her whereabouts, prompting US Special Forces to stage a daring behind-the-lines assault to pluck the brave soldier from the clutches of the enemy. She was safely returned to her family, where she could continue her dream of becoming a kindergarten teacher with the grateful support of the Army.

In the weeks and months after her rescue, a different story came to light. The story offered up by the military was a propaganda coup that would later come to symbolise the lies and tall tales that surrounded the invasion of Iraq and then Afghanistan. The community of Palestine in West Virginia didn't offer much by way of employment opportunities to the young Jessica Lynch as she contemplated her future after high school. Palestine was one of the poorer regions of West Virginia, itself one of the poorest US states, and although Lynch dreamed of working as a kindergarten teacher, the prospect of paying for a college education was difficult. When army recruiters came calling to the Lynch household in the summer of 2000, she decided to postpone her education and enroll for a spell in the military. She would get to travel, and after her military service the Army would pay for her college education. She went to basic training in Fort Jackson in South Carolina and Fort Lee in the neighbouring state of Virginia, before moving to begin work as a supply clerk with the 507th Maintenance Company in Fort Bliss in Texas.

Then came the momentous events of September 11, 2001, and the US decision to invade Iraq. In March 2003, a vast military column left Kuwait and snaked up into Iraq, headed for Baghdad, with Jessica Lynch driving one of the trucks making up the 507th Maintenance Company. Her truck broke down after a couple of days and she transferred into a Humvee, one of the army's light armoured vehicles. Made up of supply clerks, cooks and mechanics, Lynch's 507th Maintenance Company was not a fighting unit as such, but a supply and maintenance unit that travelled with a military escort. The route of the main convoy took it past the town of Nasiriyah but through a navigational error the 507th Maintenance Company unit somehow took a wrong turn and drove straight into the town. Without its military escort, the lumbering 507th Maintenance Company was an easy target and as the company commanders realised their error and tried to turn back, the unit was ambushed, taking fire from rocket-propelled grenades. Lynch's Humvee took a hit from an RPG. She was hurled to the ground inside the vehicle and was knocked unconscious, breaking bones and fracturing her spine. Eleven American soldiers were killed in the attack.

Lynch was captured by Iraqi militia forces and taken to a civilian hospital in Nasiriyah where Dr Harith al-Houssona treated her for a broken arm and thigh and a dislocated ankle. Another Iraqi, Mohammed Odeh al-Rehaief, had noted Lynch's presence in the hospital, and got word to the American forces who began planning a rescue.

On April 2, the American army released an extraordinary short film of the rescue of Jessica Lynch. The film captured the assault on the hospital by soldiers who detained hospital staff and fired shots in the process of rescuing the young American soldier and spiriting her away by helicopter. Journalists in Doha were called to a press conference thinking that Saddam Hussein had been captured. Instead they were fed the story of a young blonde American soldier who had been wounded in an ambush, fought back valiantly and then resisted interrogation and assault after being captured, before being rescued from the clutches of the Iraqis in a daring military raid. Of course, propaganda is an essential part of any war effort, and the story of Lynch's rescue was intended to boost the nation's morale. The timing of the story of Jessica Lynch's capture and subsequent rescue came two weeks into the invasion, as coalition forces were getting bogged down and the expected knockout success had failed to materialise. The *New York Times* and *Washington Post* were among the newspapers to repeat the story that Lynch had been shot in the ambush. Other newspapers took the details to a more gory extreme. The story evoked comparisons with the 1998 movie *Saving Private Ryan*, and NBC set about making a TV movie called *Saving Jessica Lynch*, based on the account of Al-Rehaief, who was granted asylum in the US. Al-Rehaief published his own account of the affair in his book *Because Each Life Is Precious*.

Yet questions began to arise suggesting that there was an element of staging to the story, though at first they came mostly from the British press. Within six weeks of Lynch's rescue, the British newspapers were suggesting that the story was suspect. The Iraqi doctor Harith Al-Hassouna told the Guardian that Lynch had been assigned the only specialist bed in the hospital and that he had protected her from Iraqi militia forces, who left the hospital seven days after the ambush. Once the forces had left, the doctor arranged to return Lynch to the American side. An ambulance carried Lynch back to her colleagues but when it approached the American lines, soldiers opened fire and Lynch was forced to return to the hospital.

Two days later, after darkness had fallen, US forces dramatically arrived to collect the soldier. The hospital staff tried to present the Americans with keys to the building and then watched in puzzlement as the US forces elected to kick down the doors instead, and ran through the building shouting and firing weapons. One of the staff imagined that the US soldiers were imitating Arnold Schwarzenegger and Jackie Chan. With the soldiers acting out an adventure movie, a military cameraman had accompanied the raid. The short film that accompanied the story glossed over the fact that the raid on a civilian hospital had encountered no resistance. Some reporters began to discern the influence of the Rendon group, and it turned out that the Washington-based PR company that inspired the film *Wag the Dog* had indeed been instrumental in writing and filming the Jessica Lynch story. They had done their work well. The story of Jessica Lynch spread across the world and the Lynch home in Palestine, West Virginia was besieged by reporters as the family found themselves inundated with offers to sell their stories to the television networks.

In reporting the story, American newspapers and networks did not cover themselves in glory in reporting the story. With much of the information being provided through leaks and off-the-record briefings, the *Washington Post*, historically close to the Pentagon, was first to report the details. The *New York Times* followed suit and assigned Jayson Blair to cover the story from the point of view of Lynch's parents. Blair turned in a report from the Lynch homestead, complete with details about the view of cattle pastures and tobacco fields from the front porch of the house. It soon transpired that Blair – who gained a reputation as a fantasist but also exposed the weak editorial oversight at the paper – had never even been to Palestine and had invented the story.

The next mythologist to pick up the thread was Rick Bragg, who had been suspended by the *New York Times*, accused of using the work of a freelancer without attribution. After resigning from the paper, Rick Bragg signed Lynch up for a tell-it-all book about the incident. In the book, *I Am A Soldier Too: The Jessica Lynch Story*, Bragg implies that Lynch sustained most of her injuries between the time of the ambush and her arrival at the hospital, and writes that she was raped during this time.

Jessica Lynch herself had no memory of begin raped, and as she convalesced, she was puzzled by the coverage of the incident in her home country. Her version of the story was fundamentally at odds with the Pentagon's original story. In an interview on ABC News in November 2003, with Bragg sitting in, Lynch explained that she had been well taken care of in the Nasiriyah hospital. She started to explain that her injuries were sustained in the crash when Bragg intervened and argued that she could not be sure what had happened as she was unconscious. Lynch said that she considered the soldiers in Iraq, and her rescuers, to be true heroes.

As the invasion moved into an occupation phase, and the US built its base in Baghdad, Lynch's story was picked apart by opponents of the military action. As searches of the Iraqi countryside failed to turn up evidence of chemical weapons and other 'weapons of mass destruction', the lies that surrounded the Jessica Lynch story seemed emblematic of the lies told in the greater public relations drive to sell the invasion to the American public.

Jessica Lynch received an honourable discharge from the Army in August of 2003 and underwent 21 surgeries over the intervening years. She still wears a brace on her leg and says that she has no feeling below the knee. She received a full scholarship to West Virginia University where she earned a degree in Elementary Education. She has called the stories propaganda. In 2013, she told

ABC news: "I had to set the record straight. I knew that, even ten years later, I would not have been able to live with myself knowing that I let those stories escalate and I went along with what those other people were saying, because I knew in my heart that that's not really what happened.... I wasn't the hero they were trying to make me out to be." Thus, Jessica Lynch entered the rare group of Lynches who claimed to be of lesser importance than their legends suggested.

THE RETURN OF LINZ

When I first visited Vienna a number of years ago, with a German colleague, I told our Austrian host that it was possible that the Lynch family had Austrian origins. We were in good company, our host remarked, observing that the country had many famous sons including Sigmund Freud, Wolfgang Amadeus Mozart, and Erwin Schroedinger. My German friend interjected drolly: "Don't forget Adolf Hitler."

Adolf Hitler planned not to be forgotten, and the Austrian city of Linz loomed large in those plans. Even as his regime drew up plans to conquer the world, Hitler had a secret plan to elevate the city he came to think of as his childhood home to a world capital. He planned to build a super museum, and place at its centre the famous *Ghent Altarpiece*, the enormous multi-panelled painting that had been forcibly repatriated from Germany to Belgium as part of the treaty of Versailles at the end of the First World War. With the *Ghent Altarpiece* in Linz, surrounded by the greatest art in the world, Hitler would right the perceived wrongs of the Versailles treaty, and make Linz the envy of Vienna and the other great world capitals.

Adolf Hitler was born in Braunau am Inn on the Austrian-German border in 1889, and after a spell living in Passau in Germany, the young Adolf returned with his family to Austria where they settled in 1894 in Leonding, on the outskirts of Linz. After a brief period in Filschling when they unsuccessfully tried their hand at farming, the family returned to Leonding and Adolf was enrolled in the school in Linz. Following the death of his father in January 1903, Adolf was enrolled in a boy's boarding house in Linz to avoid the long walk from Leonding. In September 1904 he moved to a different school, 25 miles away, and dropped out the following year at the age of sixteen. He spent the next year wandering around Linz, attending the opera and planning his career as an artist.

At the age of 17, he went to visit the city of Vienna where he was enthralled by the monumental scale of the architecture in the capital of the Hapsburg Empire, and decided to enrol in the Vienna Academy of Fine Arts. In 1908, he withdrew his remaining inheritance from the bank and went to live in Vienna, where he took the two-day exam for admission to the Academy's school of painting. The confident young artist-to-be was shocked when the Academy informed him that he had failed to pass the exam. Deflated, he returned to Linz, where his mother was dying of cancer.

The following year, he returned to Vienna where he planned to retake the exam. This time around, his test drawings were considered too poor to allow him to go forward to the exam stage. Two years of misery followed this rejection. Hitler moved out of his apartment, and ended up homeless in Vienna, sleeping on park benches before moving into a hostel for poor men, where he eked out a living carrying bags at the station and selling drawings that he copied from postcards. In 1914, he left Vienna and enrolled in the German Army. Less than 20 years later, Hitler was head of the Nazi party and the Chancellor of Germany.

He began to plot his revenge on the city of Vienna, which had thwarted his early ambitions. Hitler planned to eclipse Vienna by raising his home city of Linz up to the status of a world capital of culture, stuffed with the great artworks of Europe and beyond. Hitler established a secret unit of the army, based in Dresden, to administer the project. (The idea, as historian Noah Charney notes, was not unique. Jean-Dominique Vivant Denon, the first director of the

Louvre in Paris and Napoleon's chief art advisor, had drawn up a wish-list of items he wanted for the gallery and Napoleon's army had a unit devoted to stealing these works.) The Nazi party established the Einsatzstab Reichsleiter Rosenberg (ERR) under the command of Alfred Rosenberg, charged with appropriating cultural property for the Nazis. Hitler established his own unit in Dresden under Dr Hans Posse called the Special Commission for Linz, which was charged with collecting the art for Hitler's super-museum.

Hitler had already sketched his own plans for the museum project but he commissioned the Nazi architect Albert Speer to finalise the details. The centre of Linz would be flattened to make way for the grand project, involving an enormous museum, a hotel, theatre, opera house, parade ground and library. The architect of the Führermuseum itself, Roderick Fink, took his instructions directly from Hitler. The library would house art approved by the Nazis, such as the Teutonic and Scandanavian romantic and pastoral art of the late 19th century. Another wing of the museum would house the 'degenerate art' officially despised by the party (which later turned up in the private collections of Nazi officers).

The Special Commission set about gathering the art that would fill the museum complex. One of their first tasks involved recovering the *Ghent Altarpiece*. The 1432 painting was made of several panels, and Hitler and his henchmen became convinced that the painting contained a hidden map of the location of the great Christian relics and treasures, namely the Crown of Thorns, the Spear of Destiny and the Holy Grail. The Nazi art theft unit tracked the painting to Château de Pau in the French countryside, where the Belgian government had sent it for safe keeping. Hitler's second-in-command Hermann Göring seized the painting for his own collection, but Hitler then intercepted the painting and sent it to Bavaria for restoration.

To the dismay of the Nazis, one of the panels was missing. In

1934, a thief had removed the panel known as the Just Judges, before demanding an extravagant ransom for its return. (The panel has never been recovered.) It was a rare failure for the Special Commission for Linz. Where they could not steal or loot the desired art outright, they schemed to obtain it. In an effort to fund the collection off the government books, Hitler had ordered that proceeds of his book *Mein Kampf* be used for the purchase of works that could not be seized. The obsession with gathering and cataloguing the great art of Europe overlapped with another group, the *Ahnenerbe* or Ancestral and Heritage Research and Teaching Organisation, which was charged with proving the racial and cultural superiority of the Aryans, and with tracking down various religious and spiritual artefacts. In one instance, an *Ahnenerbe* team was dispatched to Ethiopia to look for the Ark of the Covenant (inspiring the Hollywood blockbuster *Raiders of the Lost Ark*).

For many years, Jan Vermeer's *The Artist in His Studio* was one of the most desired and sought-after paintings in Europe, though the wealthy Czernin family in Vienna refused all offers to sell the painting. The Special Commission first connived to obtain the painting by claiming it against unpaid taxes. When the revenue service ruled that the family did not owe any tax, the Special Commission found a way to compel the family to sell the painting at a modest price. Two Rembrandts were purchased from the French wine merchant Étienne Nicolas. However, few other families received payment for their treasures. Across Europe, the Special Commission looted paintings, drawings, prints, tapestries, sculptures, furniture and books. Paintings from Rembrandt, Raphael and Leonardo were looted from Poland and work by Albert Dürer, Rubens and Hans Memling were spirited southwards to Bavaria. Some of Hitler's appointees surreptitiously sold on the stolen artwork and several pieces ended up in the Linz collection through this circuitous route after being re-purchased or re-stolen.

The scale of the art theft was enormous. The ERR looted homes, libraries and universities, and even the belongings of people sent to concentration camps. Its operations reached into Belarus, Belgium, Czechoslovakia, France, Greece, Italy, the Netherlands, Norway, Poland, Lithuania and Russia. The ERR's own records showed that almost 1.5 million wagons of looted cultural property arrived to Bavaria by train, with more than four hundred thousand tons arriving by ship.

The purchased art was sorted out in Munich while the stolen art was dispatched to various castles around Bavaria for storage, while miners in Alt Aussee, a village high in the Austrian Alps, unwittingly prepared a salt mine to receive the bounty. Early in 1944, convoys began to take the cargo to their final hiding place in the salt mines, before their eventual procession to the rebuilt city of Linz. The last consignment of the 12,000 items bound for Linz arrived to the mine in April 1945, a month before the Allied forces declared victory in Europe. When Hitler retreated to his bunker in Berlin, he took with him a model of his plan for Linz and pored over it even as Berlin burned.

As the Allies closed in on Austria from all directions, August Eigruber, the administrator of the Oberdonau region, gave an order to destroy the contents of the mines to prevent the Allies from discovering the extent of the plunder, but the Austrian workmen in charge of the demolition simply walked out of the mines on hearing of the Allied approach. The entrance was sealed but the artwork was preserved.

The Allies had set up their own special department known as the Monuments, Fine Arts and Archives Program in 1943 to track culturally important artworks. Two of the 'Monuments Men', Robert Posey and Lincoln Kirstein, were hunting for the *Ghent Altarpiece* when a chance meeting changed their lives. Beset by a toothache, Posey visited a dentist in Trier in Germany who told him that his son-in-law was also an art historian. The man who was hiding in a cottage in the woods, was Hermann Bunjes, formerly one of Göring's advisors. Assuming that they already knew of the elaborate scheme, Bunjes told the astonished men about Hitler's plan for the museum at Linz, and the location of the various storage depots. On the strength of Bunjes's confession, the Monuments Men headed towards the salt mines above Alt Aussee, where the planned contents of Hitler's super-museum were spread across seven caverns. One of the first pieces they came across was the priceless *Ghent Altarpiece*, propped against the walls of the mine.

Although the Germans had assiduously catalogued all of the work, more than half of the catalogues themselves went missing. Not all of the looted art was in the Alt Aussee mines. Much of it had been stolen by Nazi officers; still more was seized by the Russians, destined for the great museums of St. Petersburg.

Shortly after the end of the war, James Plaut, head of the Art Looting Investigation Unit of the OSS (forerunner to the CIA), wrote that the upending of the Führermuseum plan put paid not just to impoverishment of cultural wealth in the countries around Germany, but also the plan to reduce all art to the Nazi formula. Parts of the haul continue to surface several decades later. A huge haul of paintings worth more than €1 billion was discovered in Munich in 2012 in the apartment of an elderly art dealer, and many of them are suspected to have come through the art theft program.

Linz had periodically enjoyed a prominence out of proportion to its size and location. The Holy Roman Emperor Friedrich III spent the last part of his life in Linz prior to his death in 1493, making the city briefly the centre of the Holy Roman Empire. Hitler's plans would have transformed Linz into a monument to Nazi art, and a tribute to Nazi superiority over its neighbours, with their precious artworks displayed across kilometres of corridors as a reminder of both its degeneracy and the inability of these countries to protect their own cultural heritage. The *Ghent Altarpiece* is once more in its rightful place, with a replica of the *Just Judges* panel making it complete, if not completely original.

Linz, meanwhile, enjoyed a spell as the European Capital of Culture in 2009, and seems happy to be known these days for its metal artwork, its electronic music festival, its Linzer Torte, and its long history on the bend of the River Danube.

MORE OF US?

So there we have 1,000 years of the Lynch family in history, myth and legend. Whether the Lynch family started out as Vikings or Austrians remains to be resolved, but certainly they were once soldiers of fortune who came to Ireland with conquering on their minds, which does tend to sway us towards the Viking/Norman angle. Always alert to new opportunities, they settled Galway and thankfully for the rest of the world, temporarily abandoned their more violent ways.

The Lynches played a role in the conquering of the Caribbean and the settlement of the Americas, north and south, and even gave their name to the horrible practice of lynching. In an unsettled USA, few would argue that racial harmony has been established, and young black men still die at the hands of authorities at a greater rate than their young white counterparts. If the world becomes be a better place, lynching may become history.

With the world population continuing to rise, there's likely to be even more Lynches around over the next generations. With luck, they'll continue to contribute to the world at a rising rate of creativity, eccentricity and surrealism. High praise indeed would be for more occasion to utter the sentiment: "It's Lynchian."

AUTHOR

Rónán Lynch is author of *The Kirwans of Castlehacket: History, folklore and mythology in an Irish horseracing family*, published by Four Courts Press. He has a PhD in History from the National University of Ireland, Galway, and is editor-in-chief at No Ordinary Life.

Made in United States
Orlando, FL
17 July 2022

19885844R00088